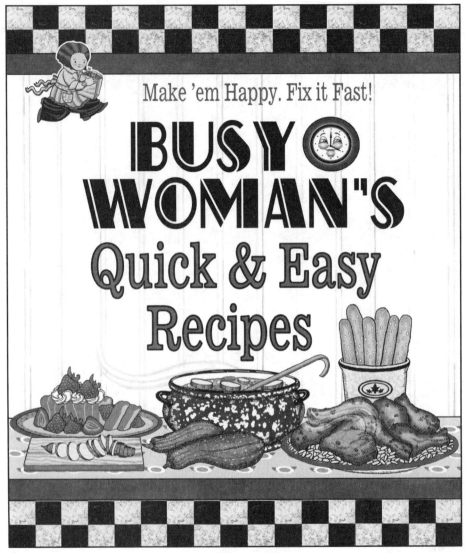

Make 'em Happy. Fix it Fast!

BUSY WOMAN'S
Quick & Easy
Recipes

Cookbook Resources LLC
Highland Village, Texas

Busy Woman's Quick & Easy Recipes
Make 'em Happy. Make It Fast!

1st Printing - March 2007
2nd Printing - March 2008
3rd Printing - September 2008
4th Printing - April 2009
5th Printing - October 2009

International Standard Book Number: 978-1-931294-23-2

Library of Congress Control Number: 2008935585

Cover and Illustrations by Nancy Bohanan

Edited, Designed, Published and Manufactured in the United States of America by
Cookbook Resources, LLC
541 Doubletree Drive
Highland Village, Texas 75077

Toll free 866-229-2665

www.cookbookresources.com

cookbook resources® LLC
Bringing Family and Friends to the Table

Busy Woman's Quick & Easy Recipes

Busy woman... kind of redundant, isn't it?

What woman isn't busy? Look around, can you find one? We couldn't either. Therefore, Cookbook Resources, LLC proudly offers you *Busy Woman's Quick & Easy Recipes*, a collection of time-saving meal ideas that will actually give busy women the opportunity to scratch one thing off that to-do list each day.

These recipes were tested for taste and ease of preparation right in our own kitchens. From appetizers to entrees or soups to desserts, this cookbook is filled with excellent meal ideas that are simple enough for the busiest of people.

We didn't just think about getting dinner together. No, ma'am! We looked at the whole picture. If a meal made a big mess in our kitchen, it didn't make the cookbook. If we couldn't locate the ingredients at our local grocery store, we didn't include them. These recipes are simple from start to finish without sacrificing one bit of flavor.

After all, a few minutes saved in the kitchen are a few more minutes to spend with your family. And that is time well spent.

Contents

Contents

Dedication

With a mission of helping you bring family and friends to the table, Cookbook Resources strives to make family meals and entertaining friends simple, easy and delicious.

We recognize the importance of a meal together as a means of building family bonds with memories and traditions that will be treasured for a lifetime. It is an opportunity to sit down with each other and share more than food.

This cookbook is dedicated with gratitude and respect for all those who show their love with homecooked meals, bringing family and friends to the table.

■ ■

■ *More and more statistical studies are finding that family* ■
■ *meals play a significant role in childhood development.* ■
■ *Children who eat with their families four or more nights* ■
■ *per week are healthier, make better grades, score higher on* ■
■ *aptitude tests and are less likely to have problems with drugs.* ■

■ ■

APPETIZERS

Appetizers Contents

Fiesta Dip

1 (15 ounce) can tamales	425 g
1 (16 ounce) can chili without beans	455 g
1 cup salsa	265 g
1 (8 ounce) package shredded sharp cheddar cheese	230 g
1 cup finely chopped onion	160 g

- Mash tamales with fork.

- Combine all ingredients in saucepan and heat to mix.

- Serve hot with crackers or chips. Serves 8 to 10.

Onion-Guacamole Dip

1 (8 ounce) carton sour cream	230 g
1 (1 ounce) packet onion soup mix	30 g
2 (8 ounce) cartons avocado dip	2 (230 g)
2 green onions with tops, chopped	
½ teaspoon crushed dill weed	2 ml

- Mix all ingredients in bowl and refrigerate.

- Serve with chips. Serves 8 to 10.

Vegetable Dip

1 (10 ounce) package frozen chopped spinach, thawed, well drained	280 g
1 bunch green onions with tops, chopped	
1 (1 ounce) packet vegetable soup mix	30 g
1 tablespoon lemon juice	15 ml
2 (8 ounce) cartons sour cream	2 (230 g)

- Squeeze spinach between paper towels to completely remove excess moisture.

- Combine all ingredients and add a little salt in bowl. (Adding several drops of hot sauce is also good.)

- Cover and refrigerate. Serve with chips. Serves 6 to 8.

Velvet Clam Dip

1 (8 ounce) and 1 (3 ounce) package cream cheese	230 g/85 g
¼ cup (½ stick) butter	60 g
2 (6 ounce) cans minced clams, drained	2 (170 g)
½ teaspoon Worcestershire sauce	2 ml

- Melt cream cheese and butter in double boiler.

- Add minced clams and Worcestershire sauce.

- Serve hot. Serves 8 to 10.

Horsey Shrimp Dip

1 (8 ounce) package cream cheese, softened	230 g
⅔ cup mayonnaise	75 g
1 tablespoon lemon juice	15 ml
3 tablespoons creamy horseradish	45 g
¼ cup chili sauce	70 g
½ teaspoon Creole seasoning	2 ml
¼ teaspoon garlic powder	1 ml
2 (8 ounce) cans shrimp, drained	2 (230 g)
2 green onions with tops, chopped	

- Combine cream cheese, mayonnaise, lemon juice, horseradish, chili sauce, Creole seasoning and garlic powder in bowl and blend well.

- Chop shrimp and onions, add to cream cheese mixture, blend and refrigerate. Serve with chips. Serves 8 to 10.

Chunky Shrimp Dip

2 (6 ounce) cans tiny cooked shrimp, drained	2 (170 g)
2 cups mayonnaise	450 g
6 green onions with tops, finely chopped	
¾ cup chunky salsa	200 g

- Crumble shrimp and stir in mayonnaise, onion and salsa in bowl.

- Refrigerate for 1 to 2 hours.

- Serve with crackers. Serves 8 to 10.

Hot Rich Crab Dip

1 (10 ounce) can cheddar cheese soup	280 g
1 (16 ounce) package cubed Mexican Velveeta® cheese	455 g
1 (6 ounce) can crabmeat, flaked, drained	170 g
1 (16 ounce) jar salsa	455 g

- Combine soup and cheese in microwave-safe bowl.

- Microwave at 1-minute intervals until cheese melts.

- Add crabmeat and salsa and mix well.

- Serve hot with chips. Serves 8 to 10.

Unbelievable Crab Dip

Don't count on your guests leaving the table until this dip is gone!

1 (16 ounce) package cubed Velveeta® cheese	455 g
2 (6 ounce) cans crabmeat, drained, flaked	2 (170 g)
1 bunch green onions with tops, chopped	
2 cups mayonnaise	450 g
½ teaspoon seasoned salt	2 ml

- Melt cheese in double boiler. Add crabmeat, onions, mayonnaise and seasoned salt.

- Serve hot or at room temperature with assorted crackers. Serves 8 to 10.

Tasty Tuna Dip

1 (6 ounce) can tuna in spring water, drained, flaked	170 g
1 (1 ounce) packet Italian salad dressing mix	30 g
1 (8 ounce) carton sour cream	230 g
¼ cup chopped black olives, drained	30 g

- Combine all ingredients in bowl and stir until they blend well. Refrigerate for 8 hours. Serve with melba rounds. Serves 6 to 8.

Crunchy Asparagus Dip

1 (14 ounce) can asparagus spears, drained, chopped	395 g
½ cup mayonnaise	110 g
¼ teaspoon hot sauce	1 ml
½ cup chopped pecans	55 g

- Combine all ingredients in medium bowl and refrigerate. Serve with wheat crackers. Serves 6.

Hot Broccoli Dip

2 (16 ounce) packages cubed Mexican Velveeta® cheese	2 (455 g)
1 (10 ounce) can golden mushroom soup	280 g
1 (10 ounce) package frozen chopped broccoli, thawed, drained	280 g

- Melt cheese with soup in saucepan and stir in broccoli. Heat thoroughly. Serve hot with chips. Serves 8 to 10.

Hot Artichoke Spread

1 (14 ounce) can artichoke hearts, drained, chopped	395 g
1 (4 ounce) can diced green chilies, drained	115 g
1 cup mayonnaise	225 g
1 cup shredded mozzarella cheese	115 g
¼ teaspoon white pepper	1 ml
½ teaspoon garlic salt	2 ml
Paprika	

- Preheat oven to 300° (150° C).

- Remove any spikes or tough leaves from artichoke hearts. Combine all ingredients in bowl and mix well.

- Place in sprayed 9-inch (23 cm) baking dish and sprinkle paprika over top.

- Bake for 30 minutes. Serve warm with tortilla chips or crackers. Serves 6 to 8.

Creamy Ham Dip

This will also make great little sandwiches on party rye bread.

2 (8 ounce) packages cream cheese, softened	2 (230 g)
2 (6 ounce) cans deviled ham	2 (170 g)
2 heaping tablespoons horseradish	40 g
¼ cup minced onion	40 g
¼ cup finely chopped celery	25 g

- Beat cream cheese in bowl until creamy.

- Stir in ham, horseradish, onion and celery.

- Refrigerate and serve with crackers. Serves 8 to 10.

Nutty Apple Dip

1 (8 ounce) package cream cheese, softened	230 g
1 cup packed brown sugar	220 g
1 teaspoon vanilla	5 ml
1 cup finely chopped pecans	110 g

- Combine cream cheese, sugar and vanilla in bowl and beat until smooth.

- Stir in pecans. Serve with sliced apples for dipping. Serves 6.

Zippy Broccoli-Cheese Dip

1 (10 ounce) package frozen chopped broccoli, thawed, drained	280 g
2 tablespoons butter	30 g
2 ribs celery, chopped	
1 small onion, finely chopped	
1 (16 ounce) package cubed mild Mexican Velveeta® cheese	455 g

- Make sure broccoli is thoroughly thawed and drained.

- Place butter in large saucepan and saute broccoli, celery and onion on medium heat for about 5 minutes. Stir several times.

- Add cheese. Heat just until cheese melts and stir constantly.

- Serve hot with chips. Serves 8.

*TIP: If you want the "zip" to be zippier, use hot Mexican Velveeta®
cheese instead of mild.*

Tuna Melt Appetizer

1 (10 ounce) package frozen chopped spinach, drained	**280 g**
2 (6 ounce) cans white tuna in water, drained, flaked	**2 (170 g)**
¾ cup mayonnaise	**170 g**
1½ cups shredded mozzarella cheese, divided	**165 g**

- Preheat oven to 350° (175° C).

- Squeeze spinach between paper towels to completely remove excess moisture.

- Combine spinach, tuna, mayonnaise and 1 cup (115 g) cheese in bowl and mix well.

- Spoon into sprayed pie pan and bake for 15 minutes.

- Remove from oven and sprinkle remaining cheese over top.

- Return to oven and bake for additional 5 minutes.

- Serve with crackers. Serves 8 to 10.

Fish like salmon, tuna and mackerel are considered fatty fish, but are thought of as healthy and nutritional. It is thought that eating fish helps prevent heart disease and even aids in preventing strokes and diseases like Alzheimer's.

Hot Sombrero Dip

2 (15 ounce) cans bean dip	2 (425 g)
1 pound lean ground beef, cooked	455 g
1 (4 ounce) can green chilies	115 g
1 cup hot salsa	265 g
1½ cups shredded Mexican Velveeta® cheese	170 g

- Preheat oven to 350° (175° C).

- Layer bean dip, ground beef, green chilies and salsa in 3-quart baking dish and top with cheese.

- Bake just until cheese melts, about 10 or 15 minutes.

- Serve with tortilla chips. Serves 8 to 10.

Party Smokies

1 cup ketchup	270 g
1 cup plum jelly	320 g
1 tablespoon lemon juice	15 ml
¼ cup mustard	60 g
2 (5 ounce) packages tiny smoked sausages	2 (145 g)

- Combine ketchup, jelly, lemon juice and mustard in saucepan, heat and mix well.

- Add sausages and simmer for 10 minutes.

- Serve hot with cocktail toothpicks. Serves 8.

Hot Cocktail Squares

1 (4 ounce) can diced green chilies	115 g
1 (3 ounce) jar bacon bits	85 g
1 (16 ounce) package shredded cheddar cheese	455 g
7 eggs	
Hot sauce	

- Preheat oven to 350° (175° C).

- Layer green chilies, bacon bits and cheese in sprayed 7 x 11-inch (18 x 28 cm) baking dish.

- Beat eggs well with fork and season with a little salt and several drops hot sauce. Pour over cheese.

- Cover and bake for 25 minutes.

- Uncover and bake for additional 10 minutes. Cut into squares and serve warm. Yields 12 squares.

Walnut-Cheese Spread

¾ cup chopped walnuts	180 ml
1 (16 ounce) package shredded cheddar cheese	455 g
3 green onions with tops, chopped	
½ - ¾ cup mayonnaise	120 ml
½ teaspoon liquid smoke	2 ml

- Roast walnuts at 250° (120° C) for 10 minutes.

- Combine all ingredients in bowl and let stand in refrigerator overnight.

- Spread on assorted crackers. Serves 8.

Speedy Chili con Queso

1 (16 ounce) package cubed Velveeta® cheese	455 g
½ cup milk	120 ml
1 (12 ounce) jar salsa, divided	340 g

- Melt cheese and milk in double boiler.

- Add about half of salsa. Taste and add more salsa as needed for desired heat!

- Serve with tortilla chips. Serves 8 to 10.

Sausage-Pineapple Bits

This "sweet and hot" combination has a delicious flavor.

1 pound link sausage, cooked, skinned	**455 g**
1 pound hot bulk sausage	**455 g**
1 (15 ounce) can crushed pineapple with juice	**425 g**
2 cups packed brown sugar	**440 g**
1 tablespoon marinade for chicken	**15 ml**

- Slice link sausage into ⅓-inch (8 mm) pieces. Shape bulk sausage into 1-inch (2.5 cm) balls.

- Brown sausage balls in skillet.

- Combine pineapple, brown sugar and marinade for chicken in large saucepan. Heat, add both sausages and simmer for 30 minutes.

- Serve from chafing dish or small slow cooker with cocktail toothpicks. Serves 12.

Sausage Bites

1 (1 pound) package hot sausage	455 g
1 (16 ounce) package shredded colby or cheddar cheese	455 g
3¾ cups biscuit mix	420 g
½ teaspoon garlic powder	2 ml

- Preheat oven to 350° (175° C).

- Combine all ingredients in bowl and knead thoroughly.

- Roll into 1-inch (2.5 cm) balls.

- Bake on baking sheet for 15 to 18 minutes or until light brown. Serves 12.

Spinach-Artichoke Dip

2 (10 ounce) packages frozen chopped spinach, thawed, drained	2 (280 g)
1 (14 ounce) jar marinated artichoke hearts, drained, finely chopped	395 g
1 cup mayonnaise	225 g
2 cups shredded mozzarella cheese	230 g
Chips	

- Squeeze spinach between paper towels to remove excess moisture.

- Combine all ingredients in bowl and mix well. Cover and refrigerate.

- Serve with chips. Serves 8 to 10.

Olive-Cheese Balls

2¼ cups shredded sharp cheddar cheese	255 g
1 cup flour	120 g
½ cup (1 stick) butter, melted	115 g
1 (5 ounce) jar green olives	145 g

- Preheat oven to 350° (175° C).

- Combine cheese and flour in bowl. Add butter and mix well.

- Cover olives with mixture and form into balls.

- Bake for about 15 minutes or until light brown. Serves 8 to 10.

Creamy Spinach-Pepper Dip

1 (10 ounce) package frozen chopped spinach, drained	280 g
1 (8 ounce) package shredded Monterey Jack cheese	230 g
1 (8 ounce) package cream cheese, softened	230 g
1 - 2 tablespoons chopped jalapenos	15 -30 ml

- Squeeze spinach between paper towels to remove excess moisture.

- Combine spinach, Monterey Jack, cream cheese and jalapenos in microwave-safe bowl and heat in microwave on MEDIUM until cheese melts. Stir several times while heating.

- Serve hot with chips or crackers. Serves 8 to 10.

Creamy Onion Dip

2 (8 ounce) packages cream cheese, softened	2 (230 g)
3 tablespoons lemon juice	45 ml
1 (1 ounce) packet onion soup mix	30 g
1 (8 ounce) carton sour cream	230 g

- Beat cream cheese in bowl until smooth.

- Add lemon juice and soup mix. Gradually fold in sour cream and blend well.

- Refrigerate and serve with chips, crackers or fresh vegetables. Serves 6 to 8.

Favorite Stand-By Shrimp Dip

2 cups tiny cooked shrimp, finely chopped	290 g
2 tablespoons horseradish	30 g
½ cup chili sauce	135 g
¾ cup mayonnaise	170 g
1 tablespoon lemon juice	15 ml

- Combine all ingredients with a few dashes salt in bowl and refrigerate. (If shrimp has been frozen, be sure to drain well.)

- Serve with cucumber or zucchini slices. Serves 6 to 8.

Crab Dip Kick

1 (8 ounce) package cream cheese, softened	230 g
3 tablespoons salsa	50 g
2 tablespoons horseradish	30 g
1 (6 ounce) can crabmeat, drained, flaked	170 g

- Beat cream cheese in bowl until creamy.

- Add salsa and horseradish and mix well.

- Stir in crabmeat and refrigerate.

- Serve with assorted crackers. Serves 6 to 8.

Creamy Cucumber Spread

1 (8 ounce) package cream cheese, softened	230 g
½ cup mayonnaise	110 g
1 teaspoon seasoned salt	5 ml
1 cup seeded, chopped cucumbers	120 g

- Beat cream cheese in bowl until creamy and add mayonnaise, seasoned salt and cucumber.

- Spread on crackers. Servers 6 to 8.

Roasted Garlic Dip

4 - 5 whole garlic cloves with peel	
Olive oil	
2 (8 ounce) packages cream cheese, softened	2 (230 g)
¾ cup mayonnaise	170 g
1 (7 or 9 ounce) jar roasted sweet red peppers,	
drained, coarsely chopped	200 or 255 g
1 bunch green onions with tops, chopped	

- Preheat oven to 400° (205° C).

- Lightly brush outside of garlic cloves with a little oil and place in shallow baking pan.

- Heat for about 10 minutes and cool.

- Press roasted garlic out of cloves.

- Beat cream cheese and mayonnaise in bowl until creamy. Add garlic, red peppers and onions and mix well. (Roasted peppers are great in this recipe, but if you want it a little spicy, add several drops of hot sauce.)

- Sprinkle with red pepper or paprika and serve with chips.
  Serves 8 to 10.

BEVERAGES

Beverages Contents

If you need a quick festive punch or a special, celebratory drink, champagne and canned fruit juices can save the day. Choose tropical flavors or bright colors. Mix two parts champagne and one or two parts juice and you have a beautiful, delightful drink in just a few minutes.

Cranberry-Pineapple Punch

1 (48 ounce) bottle cranberry juice	1.4 L
1 (46 ounce) can pineapple juice	1.4 L
½ cup sugar	100 g
2 teaspoons almond extract	10 ml
1 (2 liter) bottle ginger ale, chilled	2 L

- Combine cranberry juice, pineapple juice, sugar and almond extract in bowl and stir until sugar dissolves. Cover and refrigerate for 8 hours.

- When ready to serve, add ginger ale and stir. Serves 48.

Best Tropical Punch

1 (46 ounce) can pineapple juice	1.4 L
1 (46 ounce) can apricot nectar	1.4 L
3 (6 ounce) cans frozen limeade concentrate, thawed	3 (175 ml)
1 (3 quart) ginger ale, chilled	2.8 L

- Combine pineapple juice, apricot nectar and limeade concentrate in bowl and refrigerate.

- When ready to serve, add ginger ale. Serves 48.

Champagne Punch

1 (750 ml) bottle champagne, chilled	750 ml
1 (32 ounce) bottle ginger ale, chilled	945 ml
1 (6 ounce) can frozen orange juice concentrate	175 ml
Orange slices, optional	

- Combine champagne, ginger ale and orange juice concentrate in punch bowl and mix well.

- Serve chilled and garnish with orange slices. Serves 40.

Orange Slush

2 cups orange juice	500 ml
½ cup instant non-fat dry milk	35 g
¼ teaspoon almond extract	1 ml
8 ice cubes	

- Combine all ingredients in blender and process on high until mixture is smooth and thick.

- Serve immediately. Serves 2.

Very Special Coffee Punch

I Promise – This Will Make a Hit!
Everyone will be back for seconds!

1 (2 ounce) jar instant coffee granules	60 g
2¼ cups sugar	450 g
2 quarts half-and-half cream	1.9 L
1 (1 quart) ginger ale, chilled	945 ml
1 (1 pint) whipping cream, whipped	500 ml
½ gallon French vanilla ice cream	1.9 L

- Dissolve instant coffee in 2 quarts (1.9 L) hot water and cool. Add sugar and half-and-half cream, mix well and refrigerate.

- When ready to serve, pour coffee-sugar mixture in punch bowl, add ginger ale, whipped cream and ice cream. Let some chunks of ice cream remain. Serves 60 (4 ounce/125 ml servings).

Mexican Coffee

1 ounce Kahlua® liqueur	30 ml
1 cup hot, black brewed coffee	250 ml
Ground cinnamon	
Sweetened whipped cream	

- Pour Kahlua® and coffee into tall mug.

- Sprinkle with cinnamon and stir. Top with whipped cream. Serves 1.

Lemon-Banana Shake

1 (6 ounce) can frozen lemonade concentrate, thawed	175 ml
1 cup diced bananas	180 g
1 (1 quart) vanilla ice cream	945 ml
3 cups milk	750 ml

- Combine lemonade concentrate and bananas in bowl and beat until mixture is thick.

- For each milkshake, add 1 scoop vanilla ice cream and ¼ cup (60 ml) lemon-banana mixture in glass.

- Fill glass two-thirds full with milk and stir well.

- Top off with 1 more scoop of ice cream. Serves 6.

Hot Cranberry Cider

1½ quarts cranberry juice	1.4 L
1 (12 ounce) can frozen orange juice concentrate, thawed	355 ml
½ teaspoon cinnamon	2 ml

- Combine cranberry juice, orange juice and 1½ orange juice cans water in large saucepan. Bring to a boil to blend flavors.

- Add cinnamon and stir well. Serve hot. Serves 12.

Green Party Punch

This punch would be great for St. Patrick's Day!

1 (3 ounce) package lime gelatin	85 g
1 (6 ounce) can frozen limeade concentrate, thawed	175 ml
1 (6 ounce) can frozen lemonade concentrate, thawed	175 ml
1 (1 quart) orange juice	945 ml
1 (1 quart) pineapple juice	945 ml
1 tablespoon almond extract	15 ml
2 - 3 drops green food coloring	
1 (1 liter) ginger ale, chilled	1 L

- Dissolve lime gelatin and 1 cup (250 ml) boiling water and stir well.

- Combine dissolved gelatin, limeade, lemonade, orange juice, pineapple juice, almond extract and food coloring in 1-gallion (3.8 L) bottle and refrigerate.

- When ready to serve, add ginger ale. Serves 32.

Holiday Party Punch

The almond extract really gives this punch a special taste!

3 cups sugar	600 g
1 (6 ounce) package lemon gelatin	170 g
1 (3 ounce) can frozen orange juice concentrate, thawed	90 ml
⅓ cup lemon juice	75 ml
1 (46 ounce) can pineapple juice	1.4 L
3 tablespoons almond extract	45 ml
2 quarts ginger ale, chilled	1.9 L

- Combine sugar and 1-quart (945 ml) water in saucepan. Heat until sugar dissolves.

- Add gelatin and stir until it dissolves. Add fruit juices, 1½ quarts (1.4 L) water and almond extract and refrigerate.

- When ready to serve, place in punch bowl and add chilled ginger ale. Serves 50.

Strawberry Punch

2 (10 ounce) boxes frozen strawberries, thawed	2 (280 g)
2 (6 ounce) cans frozen pink lemonade concentrate	2 (175 ml)
2 (2 liter) bottles ginger ale, chilled	2 (2 L)

- Process strawberries through blender. Pour lemonade into punch bowl and stir in strawberries.

- Add chilled ginger ale and stir well. (It would be nice to make an ice ring out of another bottle of ginger ale.) Serves 24.

Reception Punch

4 cups sugar	800 g
5 ripe bananas, mashed	
Juice of 2 lemons	
1 (46 ounce) can pineapple juice	1.4 L
1 (6 once) can frozen orange juice concentrate, thawed	175 ml
2 quarts ginger ale, chilled	1.9 L

- Boil sugar and 6 cups (1.5 L) water in saucepan for 3 minutes and cool.

- Blend bananas with lemon juice in bowl and add pineapple and orange juice. Add sugar water. Freeze in large container.

- To serve, thaw for 1½ hours, then add ginger ale. Punch will be slushy. Serves 40.

Sparkling Punch

6 oranges, unpeeled, thinly sliced	
1 cup sugar	200 g
2 bottles (750 ml) dry white wine	2 (750 ml)
3 bottles (750 ml) sparkling wine, chilled	3 (750 ml)

- Place orange slices in large plastic or glass container and sprinkle with sugar.

- Add white wine, cover and refrigerate for at least 8 hours.

- When ready to serve, stir in sparkling wine. Serves 24.

Strawberry Smoothie

2 medium bananas, peeled, sliced	
1 pint fresh strawberries, washed, quartered	360 g
1 (8 ounce) container strawberry yogurt	230 g
¼ cup orange juice	60 ml

- Place all ingredients in blender. Process until smooth.

- Serve as is or over crushed ice. Serves 4.

Banana-Mango Smoothie

1 cup peeled, cubed ripe mango	165 g
1 ripe banana, sliced	
⅔ cup milk	150 ml
1 teaspoon honey	5 ml
¼ teaspoon vanilla	1 ml

- Arrange mango cubes in single layer on baking sheet and freeze for about 1 hour or until firm.

- Combine frozen mango, banana, milk, honey and vanilla in bowl and pour into blender.

- Process until smooth. Serves 2.

BREAKFAST, BRUNCH & BREADS

Breakfast, Brunch & Breads Contents

Breakfast & Brunch

Breads

Breakfast Bake

*This is a favorite for overnight guests and
even special enough for Christmas morning.*

1 pound hot sausage, cooked, crumbled	**455 g**
1 cup shredded cheddar cheese	**115 g**
1 cup biscuit mix	**120 g**
5 eggs, slightly beaten	
2 cups milk	**250 ml**

- Preheat oven to 350° (175° C).

- Place sausage in sprayed 9 x 13-inch (23 x 33 cm) baking dish and sprinkle with cheese.

- Combine biscuit mix, eggs and a little salt in bowl and beat well.

- Add milk to egg mixture and stir until fairly smooth. Pour over sausage mixture.

- Bake for 35 minutes. (You can mix this up the night before baking and refrigerate. To bake the next morning, add 5 minutes to cooking time.) Serves 6 to 8.

Breakfast Tacos

4 eggs
4 flour tortillas
1 cup cooked, chopped ham   140 g
1 cup shredded cheddar cheese   115 g

- Scramble eggs in skillet.

- Lay tortillas flat and spoon eggs over tortillas.

- Sprinkle with ham and cheese and roll to enclose filling.

- Place tacos in microwave-safe dish and microwave for 30 seconds or until cheese melts.

- Serve immediately. Serves 4.

Bacon-Egg Burrito

2 slices bacon, cooked, chopped
2 eggs, scrambled
¼ cup shredded cheddar cheese   30 g
1 flour tortilla

- Sprinkle bacon, eggs and cheese in middle of tortilla. (Add taco sauce or salsa, if you like.)

- Fold tortilla sides over and place seam-side down on dinner plate.

- Microwave for 30 seconds or just until mixture heats thoroughly. Serves 1.

Glazed Bacon

1 (1 pound) bacon	455 g
⅓ cup packed brown sugar	75 g
1 teaspoon flour	5 ml
½ cup finely chopped pecans	55 g

- Preheat oven to 350° (175° C).

- Arrange bacon slices close together, but not overlapping on wire rack over drip pan.

- Combine brown sugar, flour and pecans in bowl and sprinkle evenly over bacon.

- Bake for 30 minutes. Drain on paper towels. Serves 4 to 6.

Curried Fruit Medley

1 (29 ounce) can sliced peaches	820 g
2 (15 ounce) cans pineapple chunks	2 (425 g)
1 (10 ounce) jar maraschino cherries	280 g
1 cup packed brown sugar	220 g
1 teaspoon curry powder	5 ml
¼ cup (½ stick) butter, cut into pieces	60 g

- Preheat oven to 350° (175° C).

- Drain all fruit and place in 9 x 13-inch (23 x 33 cm) baking dish. Combine brown sugar and curry in bowl and stir well. Sprinkle over fruit and dot with butter.

- Cover and bake for 30 minutes or until thoroughly hot. Serves 8.

Apricot Bake

4 (15 ounce) cans apricot halves, drained, divided	4 (425 g)
1 (16 ounce) box light brown sugar, divided	455 g
2 cups round, buttery cracker crumbs, divided	120 g
½ cup (1 stick) butter, sliced	115 g

- Preheat oven to 300° (150° C).

- Place 2 cans drained apricots in sprayed 9 x 13-inch (23 x 33 cm) baking dish.

- Sprinkle half brown sugar and half cracker crumbs over apricots. Dot with half butter and repeat layers.

- Bake for 1 hour. Serves 6 to 8.

Mexican Breakfast Eggs

¼ cup (½ stick) butter	60 g
9 eggs	
3 tablespoons milk	45 ml
5 tablespoons salsa	80 g
1 cup crushed tortilla chips	90 g

- Melt butter in skillet.

- Beat eggs in bowl and add milk and salsa.

- Pour egg mixture into skillet and stir until eggs cook lightly.

- Stir in tortilla chips and serve hot. Serves 4.

Pineapple-Cheese Casserole

*This is really a different kind of recipe and very good. It can be
served at brunch and is also great with sandwiches at lunch.*

1 cup sugar	200 g
5 tablespoons flour	40 g
2 (20 ounce) cans unsweetened pineapple chunks,	
drained	2 (570 g)
1½ cups shredded cheddar cheese	170 g
1 stack round, buttery crackers, crushed	
½ cup (1 stick) butter, melted	115 g

- Preheat oven to 350° (175° C).

- Combine sugar and flour in bowl.

- Layer pineapple, sugar-flour mixture, shredded cheese and cracker
  crumbs in sprayed 9 x 13-inch (23 x 33 cm) baking dish.

- Drizzle butter over casserole.

- Bake for 25 minutes or until bubbly. Serves 6 to 8.

Ranch Sausage-Grits

1 cup quick-cooking grits	**155 g**
1 (1 pound) pork sausage	**455 g**
1 onion, chopped	
1 cup salsa	**265 g**
1 (8 ounce) package shredded cheddar cheese, divided	**230 g**

- Preheat oven to 350° (175° C).

- Cook grits according to package directions and set aside.

- Cook and brown sausage and onion in skillet and drain well.

- Combine grits, sausage mixture, salsa and half cheese and spoon into sprayed 2-quart (2 L) baking dish.

- Bake for 15 minutes.

- Remove from oven, add remaining cheese and bake for additional 10 minutes. Serve hot. Serves 4 to 6.

*This is a great dish for a Sunday night breakfast, Start
a fun family tradition with breakfast on Sunday nights.*

Cinnamon Souffle

1 loaf cinnamon-raisin bread
1 (20 ounce) can crushed pineapple with juice   **570 g**
1 cup (2 sticks) butter, melted   **230 g**
½ cup sugar   **100 g**
5 eggs, slightly beaten

- Preheat oven to 350° (175° C).

- Slice off very thin portion of bread crusts.

- Tear bread into small pieces and place in sprayed 9 x 13-inch (23 x 33 cm) baking dish.

- Pour pineapple and juice over bread and set aside.

- Cream butter and sugar in bowl.

- Add eggs to creamed mixture and mix well.

- Pour creamed mixture over bread and pineapple. Bake uncovered for 40 minutes. Serves 6 to 8.

TIP: If you have some pecans handy, ½ cup (55 g) chopped pecans really adds extra texture and flavor.

Light, Crispy Waffles

2 cups biscuit mix	**240 g**
1 egg	
½ cup canola oil	**125 ml**
1⅓ cups club soda	**325 ml**

- Preheat waffle iron.

- Combine all ingredients in bowl and stir with spoon. Pour just enough batter to cover waffle iron and cook. Serves 4.

TIP: To have waffles for a "company weekend", make them before the guests arrive. Freeze the waffles separately on a baking sheet and place in large plastic bags. To heat, bake at 350° (175° C) for about 10 minutes.

Bacon-Sour Cream Omelet

2 eggs	
5 strips bacon, fried, drained, crumbled	
⅓ cup sour cream	**80 g**
3 green onions, chopped	
1 tablespoon butter	**15 ml**

- Beat eggs with 1 tablespoon (15 ml) water in bowl. In separate bowl, combine bacon and sour cream. Saute onions in bacon drippings and mix with bacon-sour cream.

- Melt butter in omelet pan. Pour in egg mixture and cook. When omelet is set, spoon sour cream mixture along center and fold omelet onto warm plate. Serves 1.

Christmas Breakfast

12 - 14 eggs, slightly beaten	
1 pound sausage, cooked, drained, crumbled	455 g
2 cups milk	500 ml
1½ cups shredded cheddar cheese	170 g
1 (5 ounce) box seasoned croutons	145 g

- Preheat oven to 350° (175° C).

- Mix all ingredients in bowl and pour into 9 x 13-inch (23 x 33 cm) baking dish. Bake for 40 minutes.

- Let stand for about 10 minutes before serving. Serves 6 to 8.

Pineapple Coffee Cake

1 (18 ounce) box butter cake mix	510 g
½ cup canola oil	125 ml
4 eggs, slightly beaten	
1 (20 ounce) can pineapple pie filling	570 g

- Preheat oven to 350° (175° C).

- Combine cake mix, oil and eggs in bowl and beat well. Pour batter into sprayed, floured 9 x 13-inch (23 x 33 cm) baking pan.

- Bake for 45 to 50 minutes. Cake is done when toothpick inserted in center comes out clean

- Punch holes in cake about 2 inches (5 cm) apart with knife. Spread pineapple pie filling over cake while hot. Serves 8 to 10.

Cranberry Coffee Cake

2 eggs
1 cup mayonnaise   **225 g**
1 (18 ounce) box spice cake mix   **510 g**
1 (16 ounce) can whole cranberry sauce   **455 g**
Powdered sugar

- Preheat oven to 325° (165° C).

- Beat eggs, mayonnaise and cake mix in bowl and fold in cranberry sauce.

- Pour into sprayed, floured 9 x 13-inch (23 x 33 cm) baking pan.

- Bake for 45 minutes. Cake is done when toothpick inserted in center comes out clean.

- When cake is cool, dust with powdered sugar. (If you would rather have frosting than powdered sugar, use prepared frosting.) Serves 8 to 10.

Pecan Waffles

2 cups flour	240 g
½ cup canola oil	125 ml
½ cup milk	125 ml
⅔ cup finely chopped pecans	75 g

- Preheat waffle iron.

- Combine flour, oil and milk in bowl and mix well.

- Stir in chopped pecans.

- Pour approximately ¾ cup (175 ml) batter onto hot waffle iron and cook until brown and crispy. Serves 4.

Homemade Egg Substitute

6 egg whites	
¼ cup instant non-fat dry milk	15 g
2 teaspoons canola oil	10 ml
¼ teaspoon ground turmeric	1 ml

- Combine all ingredients in blender, add 2 teaspoons (10 ml) water and process for 30 seconds. Refrigerate.

Green Chile Squares

2 cups diced green chilies	480 g
1 (8 ounce) package shredded sharp cheddar cheese	230 g
8 eggs, beaten	
½ cup half-and-half cream	125 ml

- Preheat oven to 350° (175° C).

- Place green chilies in sprayed 9 x 13-inch (23 x 33 cm) baking pan and cover with cheese.

- Combine eggs, a little salt and pepper and half-and-half cream in bowl and pour over green chilies and cheese.

- Bake for 30 minutes.

- Let stand at room temperature for a few minutes before cutting into squares. Yields 12 squares.

Praline Toast

½ cup (1 stick) butter, softened	115 g
1 cup packed brown sugar	220 g
½ cup finely chopped pecans	55 g
Bread slices	

- Combine butter, brown sugar and pecans in bowl and mix well.

- Spread butter mixture on bread slices.

- Toast in broiler until brown and bubbly.

Baked Grits

2 cups quick-cooking grits	310 g
2 cups milk	500 ml
¾ cup (1½ sticks) butter	170 g
4 eggs, beaten	

- Preheat oven to 350° (175° C).

- Stir grits in 4 cups (1 L) water in saucepan over medium heat for about 5 minutes.

- Add milk and butter, cover and cook for additional 10 minutes. Remove from heat and add eggs.

- Pour in sprayed baking dish and bake for 30 minutes. Serves 6.

Peach Bake

2 (15 ounce) cans peach halves, drained	2 (425 g)
1 cup packed brown sugar	220 g
1 cup round, buttery cracker crumbs	60 g
½ cup (1 stick) butter, melted	115 g

- Preheat oven to 325° (165° C).

- Layer peaches, brown sugar and cracker crumbs in sprayed 2-quart (2 L) baking dish. Pour melted butter over casserole.

- Bake for 35 minutes or until cracker crumbs are slightly brown. Serve hot or at room temperature. Serves 4 to 6.

Garlic Toast

1 loaf French bread	
1 tablespoon garlic powder	15 ml
2 tablespoons dried parsley	30 ml
½ cup (1 stick) butter, melted	115 g
1 cup grated parmesan cheese	100 g

- Preheat oven to 225° (110° C).

- Slice bread diagonally into 1-inch (2.5 cm) slices. Combine remaining ingredients except cheese in small bowl and mix well. Brush mixture on bread and sprinkle cheese.

- Place on baking sheet and bake for about 1 hour. Serves 12.

Sour Cream Biscuits

2 cups plus 1 tablespoon flour	240 g/15 ml
1 tablespoon baking powder	15 ml
½ teaspoon baking soda	2 ml
½ cup shortening	75 g
1 (8 ounce) carton sour cream	230 g

- Preheat oven to 400° (205° C). Combine dry ingredients in bowl, add a little salt and cut in shortening.

- Gradually add sour cream and mix lightly. Turn on lightly floured board and knead a few times. Roll to ½-inch (1.2 cm) thickness. Cut with biscuit cutter and place on sprayed baking sheet.

- Bake for 15 minutes or until light brown. Serves 4 to 6.

Cheesy Herb Bread

1 loaf French bread	
½ teaspoon garlic powder	2 ml
1 teaspoon marjoram leaves	5 ml
1 tablespoon dried parsley	15 ml
½ cup (1 stick) butter, softened	115 g
1 cup grated parmesan cheese	100 g

- Preheat oven to 375° (190° C).

- Slice bread into 1-inch (2.5 cm) slices. Combine garlic powder, marjoram, parsley and butter in bowl. Spread mixture on bread slices and sprinkle with cheese.

- Wrap in foil and bake for 20 minutes. Unwrap and bake for additional 5 minutes. Serves 12.

Popovers

2 cups flour   240 g
6 eggs, beaten
2 cups milk   500 ml
Butter

- Preheat oven to 425° (220° C).

- Combine flour and 1 teaspoon (5 ml) salt in bowl. Add eggs and
  milk and mix. (The batter will be like heavy cream.)

- Coat popover pans with butter and heat in oven. Fill each cup half
  full. Bake for 20 minutes. Reduce heat to 375° (190° C) and bake
  for additional 25 minutes. Serve immediately. Serves 8.

Salad Muffins

⅓ cup sugar   70 g
⅓ cup canola oil   75 ml
¾ cup milk   175 ml
2 eggs
2 cups biscuit mix   240 g

- Preheat oven to 400° (205° C).

- Combine sugar, oil and milk in bowl. Beat in eggs and biscuit
  mix. Mix well; mixture will be a little lumpy. Pour into sprayed
  muffin pans, filling each cup two-thirds full.

- Bake for about 10 minutes or until light brown. Serves 8.

Spicy Cornbread Twists

3 tablespoons butter	45 g
⅓ cup cornmeal	55 g
¼ teaspoon cayenne pepper	1 ml
1 (11 ounce) package refrigerated soft breadsticks	310 g

- Preheat oven to 350° (175° C).

- Place butter in pie pan and melt in oven. Remove from oven.

- Mix cornmeal and red pepper on wax paper. Roll breadsticks in butter and then in cornmeal mixture.

- Twist breadsticks according to package directions and place on baking sheet. Bake for 15 to 18 minutes. Serves 6.

Souper-Sausage Cornbread

1 (10 ounce) can golden corn soup	280 g
2 eggs	
¼ cup milk	60 ml
2 (16 ounce) packages corn muffin mix	2 (455 g)
¼ pound pork sausage, cooked, drained, crumbled	115 g

- Preheat oven to 400° (205° C).

- Combine soup, eggs and milk in bowl. Stir in muffin mix just until blended. Fold in sausage. Spoon mixture into sprayed 9 x 13-inch (23 x 33 cm) baking pan.

- Bake for about 20 minutes or until light brown. Yields 12 squares.

Cream Biscuits

2 cups flour	**240 g**
3 teaspoons baking powder	**15 ml**
1 (8 ounce) carton whipping cream	**250 ml**

- Preheat oven to 375° (190° C).

- Combine flour, baking powder and ½ teaspoon (2 ml) salt in bowl.

- In separate bowl, beat whipping cream only until it holds a shape. Combine flour mixture and cream and mix with fork.

- Put dough on lightly floured board and knead about 1 minute. Pat dough to ¾-inch (1.8 cm) thickness. Cut biscuits with small biscuit cutter.

- Bake on baking sheet for about 12 minutes or until light brown. Serves 6 to 8.

Strawberry Bread

Great for finger food at parties or as sandwiches with
cream cheese and pecans — and red is always "in"!

3 cups flour	**360 g**
1 teaspoon baking soda	**5 ml**
1 teaspoon ground cinnamon	**5 ml**
2 cups sugar	**400 g**
2 (10 ounce) packages frozen strawberries, thawed	**2 (280 g)**
1¼ cups canola oil	**310 ml**
4 eggs, beaten	
1 teaspoon red food coloring	**5 ml**

- Preheat oven to 350° (175° C).

- Combine flour, baking soda, cinnamon, ½ teaspoon (2 ml) salt and sugar in bowl.

- With spoon, make a "well" in dry ingredients, add strawberries, oil and eggs and mix well. Add food coloring and mix well.

- Pour into 2 sprayed, floured loaf pans.

- Bake for 1 hour. Serves 12 to 16.

Caramel Rolls

9 tablespoons butter, softened, divided	130 g
1 cup packed light brown sugar	220 g
½ cup chopped pecans	55 g
2 (8 ounce) packages refrigerated crescent	
dinner rolls	2 (230 g)
¼ cup sugar	50 g
2 teaspoons ground cinnamon	10 ml

- Preheat oven to 375° (190° C).

- Melt 5 tablespoons (70 g) butter in 9 x 13-inch (23 x 33 cm) pan in oven. Stir in brown sugar, ¼ cup (60 ml) water and pecans and set aside.

- Separate each package of crescent rolls in 4 rectangles. Pinch perforations together to seal.

- Spread with 4 tablespoons (60 g) softened butter. Combine sugar and cinnamon in bowl and sprinkle over dough.

- Starting at shorter side, roll each rectangle and cut each roll into 4 slices, making 32 pieces. Place cut-side down in prepared pan.

- Bake for 20 to 25 minutes or until golden brown. Invert immediately to remove from pan and serve warm. Serves 8 to 10.

Orange French Toast

1 egg, beaten	
½ cup orange juice	125 ml
5 slices raisin bread	
1 cup crushed graham crackers	105 g
2 tablespoons butter	30 g

- Combine egg and orange juice in bowl. Dip bread in mixture and then in crumbs.

- Fry in butter until brown. Serves 4 to 5.

French Onion Biscuits

2 cups biscuit mix	240 g
¼ cup milk	60 ml
1 (8 ounce) container French onion dip	230 g
2 tablespoons finely minced green onion	15 g

- Preheat oven to 400° (205° C).

- Mix all ingredients in bowl until soft dough forms.

- Drop teaspoonfuls of dough onto sprayed baking sheet. Bake for 10 minutes or until light brown. Serves 6 to 8.

Apricot-Pineapple Muffins

½ cup (1 stick) butter, softened	115 g
1 cup sugar	200 g
1 egg	
1 (8 ounce) can crushed pineapple with juice	230 g
1¼ cups flour	150 g
½ teaspoon baking soda	2 ml
1 cup quick-cooking oats	80 g
⅓ cup very finely cut dried apricots	50 g

- Preheat oven to 350° (175° C).

- Cream butter and sugar in bowl, add egg and pineapple and beat well. Add all dry ingredients and ½ teaspoon (2 ml) salt, mix well and fold in apricots.

- Spoon into well sprayed muffin cups or use paper liners. Bake for 20 minutes. Yields 12 muffins.

Cheese Drops

2 cups biscuit mix	240 g
⅔ cup milk	150 ml
⅔ cup shredded sharp cheddar cheese	75 g
¼ cup (½ stick) butter, melted	60 g

- Preheat oven to 400° (205° C).

- Combine biscuit mix, milk and cheese in bowl. Drop 1 heaping tablespoon (15 ml) of dough onto sprayed baking sheet for each biscuit. Bake for 10 minutes or until light brown.

- While warm, brush tops of biscuits with melted butter. Serve hot. Serves 8.

Mozzarella Loaf

1 (16 ounce) loaf unsliced French bread	455 g
12 slices mozzarella cheese	
¼ cup grated parmesan cheese	25 g
6 tablespoons (¾ stick) butter, softened	85 g
½ teaspoon garlic salt	2 ml

- Preheat oven to 375° (190° C). Cut loaf into 1-inch (2.5 cm) thick slices. Place mozzarella slices between bread slices. Combine parmesan cheese, butter and garlic salt in bowl and spread on bread slices.

- Reshape loaf, press together and brush remaining butter mixture on outside of loaf. Bake 8 to 10 minutes. Serves 12.

Eagle Yeast Bread

8 cups flour, divided	**960 g**
1 tablespoon sugar	**15 ml**
2 yeast cakes	
1 (14 ounce) can sweetened condensed milk	**395 g**
⅓ cup canola oil	**75 ml**
Melted butter	

- Combine 6 cups (720 g) flour, sugar and 1 tablespoon (15 ml) salt in bowl and set aside.

- Soften yeast in small amount of warm water. Add sweetened condensed milk, oil and enough warm water to measure 4 cups (1 L) and mix well.

- Add to flour mixture and mix well. Add remaining 2 cups (240 g) flour and mix well.

- Knead for 10 minutes. Place in sprayed bowl.

- Let rise, covered, for 1 hour 30 minutes to 2 hours or until doubled in size.

- Divide into 3 portions. Place in 3 sprayed loaf pans. Let rise for 40 minutes.

- When ready to bake, preheat oven to 350° (175° C).

- Bake approximately for 40 minutes. Brush with melted butter. Yields 2 loaves.

Bacon-Cheese French Bread

1 (16 ounce) loaf unsliced French bread	455 g
5 slices bacon, cooked, crumbled	
1 (8 ounce) package shredded mozzarella cheese	230 g
½ cup (1 stick) butter, melted	115 g

- Preheat oven to 350° (175° C).

- Slice bread into 1-inch (2.5 cm) slices, but do not cut completely through bottom crust. Place sliced loaf on large piece of foil.

- Combine bacon and cheese in bowl and sprinkle between slices of bread. Drizzle butter over loaf and let some drip in-between slices.

- Wrap loaf tightly in foil. Bake for 20 minutes or until thoroughly hot. Serve hot. Serves 12.

Crunchy Breadsticks

1 (8 count) package hot dog buns	
1 cup (2 sticks) butter, melted	230 g
Garlic powder	
Paprika	

- Preheat oven to 225° (110° C).

- Take each half bun and slice in half lengthwise.

- Use pastry brush to butter all breadsticks. Sprinkle each breadstick lightly with garlic powder and paprika. Place on baking sheet and bake for 45 minutes. Serves 6 to 8.

Maple Syrup Biscuits

2¼ cups biscuit mix	270 g
⅔ cup milk	150 ml
1½ cups maple syrup	375 ml

- Preheat oven to 425° (220° C).

- Combine biscuit mix and milk in bowl and stir until moist. On floured surface, roll dough to ½-inch (1.2 cm) thickness. Cut out biscuits with 2-inch (5 cm) biscuit cutter.

- Pour syrup into 7 x 11-inch (18 x 28 cm) baking dish. Place biscuits on top of syrup. Bake for 13 to 15 minutes or until biscuits are golden brown. Serves 8 to 10.

Cheddar Cornbread

2 (8.5 ounce) packages corn muffin mix	2 (240 g)
2 eggs, beaten	
½ cup milk	125 ml
½ cup plain yogurt	115 g
1 (14 ounce) can cream-style corn	395 g
½ cup shredded cheddar cheese	60 g

- Preheat oven to 400° (205° C).

- Combine cornbread mix, eggs, milk and yogurt in bowl until they blend well. Stir in corn and cheese and pour into sprayed 9 x 13-inch (23 x 33 cm) baking dish.

- Bake for 18 to 20 minutes or until light brown. Yields 12 squares.

Raspberry-Filled Blueberry Muffins

1(16 ounce) box blueberry muffin mix with blueberries   455 g
1 egg
⅓ cup red raspberry jam   105 g
¼ cup sliced almonds   45 g

- Preheat oven to 375° (190° C).

- Rinse blueberries and drain.

- Combine muffin mix, egg and ½ cup (125 ml) water in bowl. Stir until moist and break up any lumps in mix.

- Place paper liners in 8 muffin cups. Fill cups half full with batter. Combine raspberry jam with blueberries in bowl and spoon mixture over batter.

- Cover with remaining batter and sprinkle almonds over batter. Bake for 18 minutes or until light brown. Yields 8 muffins.

Ham & Cheese Bars

2 cups biscuit mix	240 g
1 heaping cup cooked, finely chopped ham	160 g
1 cup shredded cheddar cheese	115 g
½ onion, finely chopped	
½ cup grated parmesan cheese	50 g
¼ cup sour cream	60 g
1 teaspoon garlic powder	5 ml
1 cup milk	250 ml
1 egg	

- Preheat oven to 350° (175° C).

- Combine all ingredients and ½ teaspoon (2 ml) salt in bowl and mix with spoon.

- Spread in sprayed 9 x 13-inch (23 x 33 cm) baking pan. Bake for 30 minutes or until light brown.

- Cut in rectangles, about 2 x 1 inch (2 x 2.5 cm). Serve hot or room temperature. Serves 6 to 8.

TIP: This is not exactly a casserole, but it goes well with a lot of our brunch casseroles. They can be served at brunch or lunch and they can be kept in the refrigerator (cooked) and reheated. To reheat, place in a 325° (165° C) oven for about 15 minutes. They will be good and crispy when reheated.

SOUPS & SALADS

Soups & Salads Contents

Broccoli-Wild Rice Soup

This is a hearty and delicious soup that is full of flavor.

1 (6 ounce) package chicken-flavored wild rice mix	170 g
1 (10 ounce) package frozen chopped broccoli, thawed	280 g
2 teaspoons dried minced onion	10 ml
1 (10 ounce) can cream of chicken soup	280 g
1 (8 ounce) package cream cheese, cubed	230 g

- Combine rice, rice seasoning packet and 6 cups (1.5 L) water in large saucepan.

- Bring to boil, reduce heat, cover and simmer for 10 minutes; stir once. Stir in broccoli and onion and simmer for 5 minutes.

- Stir in soup and cream cheese. Cook and stir until cheese melts. Serves 4 to 6.

Navy Bean Soup

3 (16 ounce) cans navy beans with liquid	3 (455 g)
1 (14 ounce) can chicken broth	395 g
1 cup chopped ham	140 g
1 large onion, chopped	
½ teaspoon garlic powder	2 ml

- Combine all ingredients in large saucepan, add 1 cup (250 ml) water and bring to a boil. Simmer until onion is tender-crisp

- Serve hot with cornbread. Serves 4 to 6.

Tomato-French Onion Soup

1 (10 ounce) can tomato bisque soup   280 g
2 (10 ounce) cans French onion soup   2 (280 g)
Croutons
Grated parmesan cheese

- Combine soups with 2 soup cans water in soup pot and heat thoroughly.

- To serve, pour soup into individual bowls and top with croutons and cheese. Serves 3 to 4.

Easy Potato Soup

1 (16 ounce) package frozen hash-brown potatoes   455 g
1 cup chopped onion   160 g
1 (14 ounce) can chicken broth   395 g
1 (10 ounce) can cream of celery soup   280 g
1 (10 ounce) can cream of chicken soup   280 g
2 cups milk   500 ml

- Combine potatoes, onion and 2 cups (500 ml) water in soup pot and bring to a boil. Cover, reduce heat and simmer for 30 minutes.

- Stir in broth, soups and milk and heat thoroughly. (If you like, garnish with shredded cheddar cheese or cooked, diced ham.) Serves 6.

Cream of Zucchini Soup

1 pound fresh zucchini, grated	455 g
1 onion, chopped	
1 (14 ounce) can chicken broth	395 g
½ teaspoon basil	2 ml
2 cups half-and-half cream, divided	500 ml

- Combine zucchini, onion, broth, basil and a little salt and pepper in soup pot.

- Bring to a boil, simmer until soft, pour into food processor and puree.

- Gradually add ½ cup (125 ml) half-and-half cream and blend. (You could add ¼ teaspoon (1 ml) curry powder, if you like curry flavor.)

- Return zucchini mixture to saucepan and add remaining half-and-half cream. Heat but do not boil. Serves 4 to 6.

When you're pouring soup or stew from one
container to another, pour it over the back of
a large spoon. The spoon will reduce splattering
and the process will be neater with less cleanup.

Fast Fiesta Soup

1 (15 ounce) can Mexican stewed tomatoes	425 g
1 (15 ounce) can whole kernel corn	425 g
1 (15 ounce) can pinto beans with liquid	425 g
2 (14 ounce) cans chicken broth	2 (395 g)
1 (10 ounce) can fiesta nacho cheese soup	280 g
1 (12 ounce) can chicken breast with liquid	340 g

- Combine tomatoes, corn, beans, broth and nacho soup in large soup pot. Heat for 10 minutes over medium heat and mix well.

- Stir in chicken with liquid and heat until thoroughly hot. Serves 6.

Southwestern Soup

1½ pounds lean ground beef	680 g
1 large onion, chopped	
2 (15 ounce) cans pinto beans with liquid	2 (425 g)
1 (15 ounce) can Ranch Style® beans, drained	425 g
2 (15 ounce) cans whole kernel corn with liquid	2 (425 g)
2 (15 ounce) cans Mexican stewed tomatoes	2 (425 g)
2 (1 ounce) packets taco seasoning mix	2 (30 g)

- Brown beef and onion in large soup pot, stir until beef crumbles and drain. Add beans, corn, tomatoes and 1½ cups (375 ml) water.

- Bring to a boil, reduce heat and stir in taco seasoning mix. Simmer for 25 minutes. Serves 8.

Speedy Vegetable Soup

1 (1 pound) lean ground beef	455 g
2 (15 ounce) cans stewed tomatoes	2 (425 g)
3 (14 ounce) cans beef broth	3 (395 g)
1 (16 ounce) package frozen mixed vegetables	455 g
½ cup instant brown rice	50 g

- Brown beef in skillet and stir until beef crumbles. Transfer to soup pot and add tomatoes, beef broth and vegetables.

- Bring to a boil, reduce heat and simmer for 20 minutes and stir occasionally. Add brown rice and cook on medium heat for 5 minutes. Serves 8.

Meatball Soup

1 (18 ounce) package frozen cooked Italian meatballs	510 g
2 (14 ounce) cans beef broth	2 (395 g)
2 (15 ounce) cans Italian stewed tomatoes	2 (425 g)
1 (16 ounce) package frozen stew vegetables	455 g

- Place meatballs, beef broth and tomatoes in large saucepan. Bring to a boil, reduce heat and simmer for 10 minutes or until meatballs are thoroughly hot. Add vegetables and cook on medium heat for 10 minutes. Serves 6 to 8.

TIP: For thicker soup, mix 2 tablespoons (15 g) cornstarch in ¼ cup (60 ml) water. Add to soup, bring to a boil, reduce heat and simmer and stir until soup thickens.

Chicken-Broccoli Chowder

2 (14 ounce) cans chicken broth	2 (395 g)
1 bunch green onions, finely chopped, divided	
1 (10 ounce) package frozen chopped broccoli	280 g
1½ cups mashed potato flakes	90 g
2½ cups cooked, cut-up chicken breasts	350 g
1 (8 ounce) package shredded mozzarella cheese	230 g
1 (8 ounce) carton whipping cream	250 ml
1 cup milk	250 ml

- Combine broth, half green onions and broccoli in large saucepan. Bring to a boil, reduce heat, cover and simmer for 5 minutes.

- Stir in potato flakes and mix until they blend well. Add chicken, cheese, cream, milk, 1 cup (250 ml) water and a little salt and pepper. Heat over medium heat and stir occasionally until hot and cheese melts, about 5 minutes.

- Ladle into individual soup bowls and garnish with remaining chopped green onions. Serves 8.

Creamy Turkey Soup

3 (14 ounce) cans chicken broth	3 (395 g)
1 pound russet potatoes, peeled, cubed	455 g
3 ribs celery, sliced	
1 (15 ounce) can sliced carrots, drained	425 g
1 (10 ounce) package frozen yellow squash	280 g
2 teaspoons minced garlic	10 ml
1 teaspoon dried thyme	5 ml
1½ cups shredded turkey	210 g
1 (10 ounce) can cream of chicken soup	280 g
1 cup milk or half-and-half cream	250 ml

- Combine chicken broth, ½ cup (125 ml) water, potatoes and celery in soup pot and bring to a boil. Add a little salt and pepper and cook on medium heat for about 20 minutes or until potatoes and celery are tender. Add carrots, squash, garlic and thyme and simmer for additional 10 minutes.

- Stir in shredded turkey, chicken soup and milk; heat just until soup is thoroughly hot, but do not boil. Serves 8.

Across-the-Border Tamale Soup

1 pound lean ground beef	455 g
1 (16 ounce) package frozen chopped onions and	
bell peppers	455 g
2 tablespoons canola oil	30 ml
1 (10 ounce) package frozen corn	280 g
2 (14 ounce) cans beef broth	2 (395 g)
1 (15 ounce) can pinto beans with liquid	425 g
2 tablespoons chili powder	30 ml
1 teaspoon ground cumin	5 ml
1 (28 ounce) can tamales, shucked, quartered	
with liquid	795 g

- Brown beef and onions and bell peppers in oil in large skillet.

- Transfer to soup pot and add corn, broth, beans, chili powder, cumin and a little salt and pepper.

- Bring to a boil, reduce heat and simmer for 30 minutes. About 15 minutes prior to serving, add tamale chunks and heat thoroughly. Stir gently so tamales will not break. Serve hot. Serves 8.

TIP: *For a spicier soup, you could add 1 (10 ounce/280 g) can tomatoes and green chilies.*

Potato-Sausage Soup

1 pound pork sausage links	**455 g**
1 cup chopped celery	**100 g**
1 cup chopped onion	**160 g**
2 (10 ounce) cans potato soup	**2 (280 g)**
1 (14 ounce) can chicken broth	**395 g**

- Cut sausage into 1-inch (2.5 cm) diagonal slices. Brown sausage in large heavy soup pot, drain and place in separate bowl. Leave about 2 tablespoons (30 ml) sausage drippings in skillet and saute celery and onion.

- Add potato soup, ¾ cup (175 ml) water, chicken broth and sausage. Bring to a boil, reduce heat and simmer for 20 minutes. Serves 4.

Blue Norther Stew

*Cold fronts in the south are called northers. This
is a great choice for one of those cold winter days.*

1½ pounds lean ground beef	680 g
1 onion, chopped	
1 (1 ounce) packet taco seasoning mix	30 g
1 (1 ounce) packet ranch dressing mix	30 g
1 (15 ounce) can whole kernel corn, drained	425 g
1 (15 ounce) can kidney beans with liquid	425 g
2 (15 ounce) cans pinto beans	2 (425 g)
2 (15 ounce) cans Mexican stewed tomatoes	2 (425 g)
1 (10 ounce) can tomatoes and green chilies	280 g

- Brown ground beef and onion in large soup pot. Add both packets seasonings and mix well.

- Add corn, beans, stewed tomatoes, tomatoes and green chilies, and 1 cup (250 ml) water, mix well and simmer for about 30 minutes. Serves 8.

*A real time-saver is to make a large pot of soup or stew and
freeze it in portions in large plastic bags. Freeze enough for
one, two or four. When the bag is sealed, it will lay flat in
the freezer and won't take up as much room as containers.
Be sure to leave a little room for expansion as it freezes.*

Beefy Bean Chili

2 pounds lean ground beef	910 g
3 ribs celery, sliced	
1 onion, chopped	
1 bell pepper, seeded, chopped	
2 teaspoons minced garlic	10 ml
1 (15 ounce) can tomato sauce	425 g
3 tablespoons chili powder	45 ml
2 (15 ounce) cans pinto beans with liquid	2 (425 g)
1 - 2 cups crushed tortilla chips	90 - 175 g

- Brown and cook ground beef in large soup pot over medium heat until meat crumbles. Add celery, onion, bell pepper and minced garlic. Cook for 5 minutes or until vegetables are tender, but not brown.

- Stir in tomato sauce, chili powder, 2 cups (500 ml) water and a little salt and pepper and mix well. Bring mixture to a boil, reduce heat and simmer for 35 minutes.

- Add beans during last 15 minutes of cooking time. Ladle into individual serving bowls and top each serving with several tablespoons crushed tortilla chips. Serves 6.

Hearty Bean and Ham Soup

What a great supper for a cold winter night!

1 (15 ounce) can sliced carrots, drained	425 g
1 cup chopped celery	100 g
1 cup chopped green bell pepper	150 g
¼ cup (½ stick) butter	60 g
2 - 3 cups cooked, diced ham	280 - 420 g
2 (15 ounce) cans navy beans with liquid	2 (425 g)
2 (15 ounce) cans jalapeno pinto beans with liquid	2 (425 g)
2 (14 ounce) cans chicken broth	2 (395 g)
2 teaspoons chili powder	10 ml

- Cook carrots, celery and bell pepper in soup pot with butter for about 8 minutes until tender-crisp.

- Add diced ham, navy beans, pinto beans, chicken broth, chili powder and a little salt and pepper. Boil and stir constantly for 3 minutes. Reduce heat and simmer for 15 minutes. Serves 8.

TIP: *Cornbread is great with this and it's so quick and easy to make. If you want to fix it, just buy 2 (8 ounce/230 g) packages corn muffin mix. Add 2 eggs and ⅔ cup (150 ml) milk, mix it up and pour it into sprayed 7 x 11-inch (18 x 28 cm) baking pan. Bake according to package directions.*

Soup with an Attitude

1 (32 ounce) carton chicken broth	910 g
3 baked potatoes, peeled, grated	
2 onions, finely chopped	
3 ribs celery, sliced	
1 (8 ounce) can green peas, drained	230 g
1 (7 ounce) can green chilies	200 g
3 cups chopped ham	420 g
1 (16 ounce) package cubed Mexican Velveeta® cheese	455 g
1 (1 pint) half-and-half cream	500 ml

- Combine broth, potatoes, onions, celery, peas, green chilies and ham in soup pot. While stirring, bring to a boil, reduce heat to medium-low and simmer for 30 minutes.

- Add cheese and stir constantly on medium heat until cheese melts. Stir in half-and-half cream and continue cooking until soup is thoroughly hot; do not boil. Serves 8.

You can save some time by slicing or chopping vegetables all at one time, then storing them in plastic bags in the refrigerator. When you're ready to use them, just pull out the bag and use what you need. You'd be surprised how nice and convenient it is.

Cabbage-Ham Soup

1 (16 ounce) package cabbage slaw	455 g
1 onion, chopped	
1 red bell pepper, seeded, chopped	
1 teaspoon minced garlic	5 ml
2 (14 ounce) cans chicken broth	2 (395 g)
1 (15 ounce) can stewed tomatoes	425 g
2 cups cooked, cubed ham	280 g
¼ cup packed brown sugar	55 g
2 tablespoon lemon juice	30 ml

- Combine cabbage, onion, bell pepper, garlic, chicken broth and 1 cup (250 ml) water in large, heavy soup pot. Bring to a boil, reduce heat and simmer for 20 minutes.

- Stir in tomatoes, ham, 1 teaspoon (5 ml) salt, brown sugar, lemon juice and a little pepper. Heat just until soup is thoroughly hot. Serves 6.

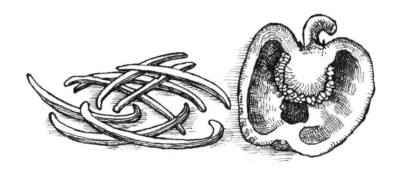

Ham and Corn Chowder

3 medium potatoes, cubed	
2 (14 ounce) cans chicken broth, divided	2 (395 g)
2 ribs celery, chopped	
1 onion, chopped	
Canola oil	
¼ cup flour	30 g
1 (1 pint) half-and-half cream	500 ml
½ teaspoon cayenne pepper	2 ml
1 (15 ounce) can whole kernel corn	425 g
1 (15 ounce) can cream-style corn	425 g
3 cups cooked, cubed ham	420 g
1 (8 ounce) package shredded Velveeta® cheese	230 g

- Cook potatoes with 1 can chicken broth in saucepan. Saute celery and onion in large soup pot with a little oil.

- Add flour and mix well on medium heat. Add second can broth and half-and-half cream. Cook, stirring constantly, until mixture thickens.

- Add potatoes, cayenne pepper, corn, cream-style corn, ham, cheese and a little salt and pepper. Heat slowly and stir several times to keep from sticking. Serves 8.

Rich Corn Chowder

8 ears fresh corn	
8 slices bacon	
1 small onion, chopped	
½ red bell pepper, seeded, chopped	
1 small baking potato, peeled, cubed	
1 (1 pint) half-and-half cream, divided	500 ml
2 teaspoons sugar	10 ml
½ teaspoon dried thyme	2 ml
1 tablespoon cornstarch	15 ml

- Cut corn from cobs into large bowl and scrape well to remove all milk.

- Fry bacon in large soup pot over medium heat, remove bacon and save drippings in pan. Crumble bacon and set aside.

- Cook onion and bell pepper in drippings until tender. Stir in corn, potato, 1 cup (250 ml) water and a little salt and pepper. Bring to boil, cover, reduce heat and simmer for 15 minutes, stirring occasionally.

- Stir in 1½ cups (375 ml) half-and-half cream, sugar and thyme.

- Combine cornstarch and remaining cream in bowl and stir until smooth. Gradually add to corn mixture and stir constantly.

- Cook uncovered for 15 minutes, stirring constantly, until soup thickens. Serves 8.

Sausage-Vegetable Soup

1 pound bulk Italian sausage	455 g
2 onions, chopped	
2 teaspoons minced garlic	10 ml
1 (1 ounce) packet beefy soup mix	30 g
1 (15 ounce) can sliced carrots, drained	425 g
2 (15 ounce) cans Italian stewed tomatoes	2 (425 g)
2 (15 ounce) cans garbanzo beans, drained	2 (425 g)
1 cup elbow macaroni	105 g

- Brown sausage, onions and garlic in large soup pot. Drain and add 4 cups (1 L) water, soup mix, carrots, tomatoes and garbanzo beans. Bring to a boil, reduce heat and simmer for 25 minutes.

- Add elbow macaroni and continue cooking for additional 15 to 20 minutes or until macaroni is tender. Serves 6.

Clam Chowder

1 (10 ounce) can New England clam chowder	280 g
1 (10 ounce) can cream of celery soup	280 g
1 (10 ounce) can cream of potato soup	280 g
1 (6 ounce) can chopped clams	170 g
1 (10 ounce) soup can milk	295 ml

- Combine all ingredients in saucepan. Heat and stir. Serves 6.

Super Easy Gumbo

1 (10 ounce) can pepper-pot soup	280 g
1 (10 ounce) can chicken gumbo soup	280 g
1 (6 ounce) can white crabmeat, flaked	170 g
1 (6 ounce) can tiny shrimp, drained	170 g

- Combine all ingredients with 1½ soup cans water in saucepan.

- Cover and simmer for 15 minutes. Serves 4.

Seafood Bisque

¼ cup (½ stick) butter	60 g
1 (8 ounce) package frozen salad shrimp, thawed	230 g
1 (6 ounce) can crabmeat, drained, flaked	170 g
1 (15 ounce) can whole new potatoes, drained, sliced	425 g
1 teaspoon minced garlic	5 ml
½ cup flour	60 g
2 (14 ounce) cans chicken broth	2 (395 g)
1 cup half-and-half cream	250 ml

- Melt butter in large saucepan. Add shrimp, crab, new potatoes and garlic and cook on medium heat for 10 minutes.

- Stir in flour and cook, stirring constantly, for 3 minutes. Gradually add chicken broth, cook and stir until mixture thickens.

- Stir in half-and-half cream and a little salt and pepper, stirring constantly and cook just until mixture is thoroughly hot; do not boil. Serves 6.

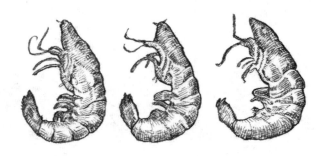

Fresh Oyster Stew

2 pints fresh oysters with liquor	1 kg
3 slices bacon	
1 small onion, chopped	
2 ribs celery, chopped	
1 (4 ounce) can sliced mushrooms	115 g
1 (10 ounce) can cream of potato soup	280 g
3 cups half-and-half cream	750 ml
⅓ cup fresh chopped parsley	20 g

- Drain oysters and save liquor. Fry bacon in skillet until crisp, drain bacon and crumble. Set aside.

- Cook onion and celery in bacon fat on medium heat until tender.

- Add mushrooms, soup, oyster liquor, half-and-half cream and a little salt and pepper. Heat over medium heat, stirring occasionally, until mixture is thoroughly hot.

- Stir in bacon and oysters and heat 4 to 5 minutes longer or until edges of oysters begin to curl. Sprinkle with parsley. Serves 6 to 8.

Incredible Broccoli-Cheese Soup

This really is an incredible soup!

1 (10 ounce) package frozen chopped broccoli	280 g
3 tablespoons butter	45 g
¼ onion, finely chopped	
¼ cup flour	30 g
1 (1 pint) carton half-and-half cream	500 ml
1 (14 ounce) can chicken broth	395 g
⅛ teaspoon cayenne pepper	.5 ml
1 (8 ounce) package mild Mexican Velveeta® cheese, cubed	115 g

- Punch several holes in broccoli package and microwave for 5 minutes. Turn package in microwave and cook for additional 4 minutes. Leave in microwave for 3 minutes.

- Melt butter in large saucepan and saute onion, but do not brown. Add flour, stir and gradually add half-and-half cream, chicken broth, ½ teaspoon (2 ml) salt, ⅛ teaspoon (.5 ml) pepper and cayenne pepper. Stir constantly and heat until mixture is slightly thick. Do not let mixture boil!

- Add cheese, stir constantly and heat until cheese melts. Add cooked broccoli. Serve piping hot. Serves 4 to 6.

Southwestern Bean Soup

Don't let the number of ingredients discourage you.
Ask yourself this question, "Can I open cans?"

¼ cup (½ stick) butter	60 g
1 onion, chopped	
1 bell pepper, seeded, chopped	
2 teaspoons minced garlic	10 ml
2 (15 ounce) cans Mexican stewed tomatoes	2 (425 g)
1 (15 ounce) can pinto beans, drained	425 g
1 (15 ounce) can kidney beans, rinsed, drained	425 g
1 (15 ounce) can black beans, rinsed, drained	425 g
1 tablespoon chili powder	15 ml
¼ teaspoon ground coriander	1 ml
1 cup shredded Mexican 4-cheese blend	115 g
1 cup shredded Monterey Jack, divided	115 g

- Melt butter in large saucepan on medium heat and cook onion, bell pepper and garlic for 5 minutes. Stir in tomatoes, beans, chili powder, coriander and a little salt and pepper.

- Bring to a boil, reduce heat, cover and simmer for 25 minutes.

- Stir in Mexican cheese and cook over low heat, stirring occasionally, just until cheese melts.

- Ladle into individual soup bowls and sprinkle Jack cheese over each serving. Serves 8.

Italian Minestrone

1 (16 ounce) package frozen onions and bell peppers	455 g
3 ribs celery, chopped	
2 teaspoons minced garlic	10 ml
¼ cup (½ stick) butter	60 g
2 (15 ounce) cans diced tomatoes	2 (425 g)
1 teaspoon dried oregano	5 ml
1 teaspoon dried basil	5 ml
2 (14 ounce) cans beef broth	2 (395 g)
2 (15 ounce) cans navy beans	2 (425 g)
2 medium zucchini, cut in half lengthwise, sliced	
1 cup elbow macaroni	105 g

- Saute onions and bell peppers, celery, and garlic in butter in soup pot for about 2 minutes. Add tomatoes, oregano, basil and a little salt and pepper. Bring to a boil, reduce heat and simmer for 15 minutes, stirring occasionally.

- Stir in beef broth, beans, zucchini and macaroni and bring to a boil. Reduce heat and simmer for additional 15 minutes or until macaroni is tender. Serves 8.

Broccoli-Noodle Salad

1 cup slivered almonds, toasted	170 g
1 cup sunflower seeds, toasted	130 g
2 (3 ounce) packages chicken-flavored ramen noodles	2 (85 g)
1 (16 ounce) package broccoli slaw	455 g
1 (8 ounce) bottle Italian salad dressing	250 ml

- Preheat oven to 300° (150° C).

- Toast almonds and sunflower seeds in oven at for about 10 minutes.

- Break up ramen noodles and mix with slaw, almonds and sunflower seeds in bowl. Toss with Italian salad dressing and refrigerate. Serves 10.

Winter Salad

1 (15 ounce) can cut green beans, drained	425 g
1 (15 ounce) can green peas, drained	425 g
1 (15 ounce) can whole kernel corn, drained	425 g
1 (15 ounce) can jalapeno black-eyed peas, drained	425 g
1 (8 ounce) bottle Italian salad dressing	230 g

- Combine all vegetables in large bowl. (Add chopped onion and chopped bell pepper if you have it handy.)

- Pour Italian dressing over vegetables. Cover and refrigerate. Serves 6 to 8.

Nutty Green Salad

6 cups torn mixed salad greens	300 g
1 medium zucchini, sliced	
1 (8 ounce) can sliced water chestnuts, drained	230 g
½ cup peanuts	75 g
⅓ cup Italian salad dressing	75 ml

- Toss greens, zucchini, water chestnuts and peanuts in bowl.

- When ready to serve, add salad dressing and toss. Serves 6 to 8.

Green and Red Salad

4 cups torn mixed salad greens	200 g
3 green onions with tops, chopped	
2 medium red apples, diced	
1 cup fresh raspberries	125 g
½ cup poppy seed dressing	125 ml

- Toss salad greens, onions and fruit in bowl.

- Drizzle with dressing and toss. Serves 6.

Special Rice Salad

1 (6 ounce) package chicken-flavored rice and macaroni	170 g
¾ cup chopped green bell pepper	110 g
1 bunch green onions with tops, chopped	
2 (6 ounce) jars marinated artichoke hearts	2 (170 g)
½ - ⅔ cup mayonnaise	110 - 150 g

- Cook rice and macaroni according to directions (but with no butter), drain and cool.

- Add green pepper, green onions, artichoke hearts and mayonnaise, toss and refrigerate. Serves 8 to 10.

Chicken Salad

3 cups boneless, skinless chicken breast halves, cooked, chopped	420 g
1½ cups chopped celery	150 g
½ cup sweet pickle relish	125 g
2 eggs, hard-boiled, chopped	
¾ cup mayonnaise	170 g

- Combine all ingredients in bowl and sprinkle with salt and pepper. Serves 6.

Fantastic Fruit Salad

2 (11 ounce) cans mandarin oranges	2 (310 g)
2 (15 ounce) cans pineapple chunks	2 (425 g)
1 (16 ounce) carton frozen strawberries, thawed	455 g
1 (20 ounce) can peach pie filling	570 g
1 (20 ounce) can apricot pie filling	570 g

- Drain oranges, pineapple and strawberries.

- Combine all ingredients in bowl and fold together gently. Serves 12 to 16.

TIP: If you have several bananas, add them too.

Peachy Fruit Salad

2 (20 ounce) cans peach pie filling	2 (570 g)
1 (20 ounce) can pineapple chunks, drained	570 g
1 (11 ounce) can mandarin oranges, drained	310 g
1 (8 ounce) jar maraschino cherries, drained	230 g
1 cup miniature marshmallows	45 g

- Combine all ingredients in large bowl, fold together gently and refrigerate.

- Serve in pretty crystal bowl. (Bananas may be added if you like.) Serves 8 to 10.

Cherry Salad

1 (20 ounce) can cherry pie filling	570 g
1 (20 ounce) can crushed pineapple, drained	570 g
1 (14 ounce) can sweetened condensed milk	395 g
1 cup miniature marshmallows	45 g
1 cup chopped pecans	110 g
1 (8 ounce) carton whipped topping, thawed	230 g
Red food coloring	

- Combine pie filling, pineapple, sweetened condensed milk, marshmallows and pecans in large bowl.

- Fold in whipped topping, refrigerate and serve in pretty crystal bowl. Add a couple drops of red food coloring for a brighter color. Serves 10.

Butter Mint Salad

1 (6 ounce) box lime gelatin	170 g
1 (20 ounce) can crushed pineapple with juice	570 g
½ (10 ounce) bag miniature marshmallows	½ (280 g)
1 (8 ounce) carton whipped topping, thawed	230 g
1 (8 ounce) bag butter mints, crushed	230 g

- Pour gelatin over pineapple in bowl. Add marshmallows and refrigerate overnight.

- Fold in whipped topping and butter mints. Pour into 9 x 13-inch (23 x 33 cm) dish and freeze. Serves 9 to 12.

Divinity Salad

1 (6 ounce) package lemon gelatin	170 g
1 (8 ounce) package cream cheese, softened	230 g
¾ cup chopped pecans	85 g
1 (15 ounce) can crushed pineapple with juice	425 g
1 (8 ounce) carton whipped topping, thawed	230 g

- Blend gelatin with 1 cup (250 ml) boiling water in bowl until it dissolves.

- Add cream cheese, beat slowly and increase speed until smooth. Add pecans and pineapple and cool in refrigerator until nearly set. Fold in whipped topping. Pour into 9 x 13-inch (23 x 33 cm) dish and refrigerate. Serves 12.

Cherry Cranberry Salad

1 (6 ounce) package cherry gelatin	170 g
1 (20 ounce) can cherry pie filling	570 g
1 (16 ounce) can whole cranberry sauce	455 g

- Combine cherry gelatin and 1 cup (250 ml) boiling water in bowl and mix until gelatin dissolves.

- Mix pie filling and cranberry sauce with gelatin.

- Pour into 9 x 13-inch (23 x 33 cm) dish and refrigerate. Serves 8.

Deviled Eggs

6 eggs, hard-boiled
2 tablespoons sweet pickle relish   **30 g**
3 tablespoons mayonnaise   **40 g**
½ teaspoon mustard   **2 ml**
Paprika

- Peel eggs and cut in half lengthwise.

- Remove yolks and mash with fork in bowl.

- Add relish, mayonnaise and mustard to yolks and place yolk mixture back into egg white halves.

- Sprinkle with paprika. Serves 6.

Sunshine Salad

2 (15 ounce) cans Mexicorn®, drained   **2 (425 g)**
2 (15 ounce) cans green peas, drained   **2 (425 g)**
1 (15 ounce) can kidney beans, rinsed, drained   **425 g**
1 (8 ounce) bottle Italian salad dressing   **250 ml**

- Combine corn, peas and beans in large bowl.

- Pour dressing over vegetables and refrigerate for several hours before serving. Serves 6.

Carrot Salad

3 cups finely grated carrots	330 g
1 (8 ounce) can crushed pineapple, drained	230 g
¼ cup flaked coconut	20 g
1 tablespoon sugar	15 ml
⅓ cup mayonnaise	75 g

- Combine carrots, pineapple, coconut and sugar in bowl and mix well. Toss with mayonnaise and refrigerate. Serves 6.

Swiss Salad

1 large head romaine lettuce	
1 bunch green onions with tops, chopped	
1 (8 ounce) package shredded Swiss cheese	230 g
½ cup toasted sunflower seeds	65 g

- Tear lettuce into bite-size pieces in bowl. Add onions, cheese and sunflower seeds and toss.

- Serve with vinaigrette salad dressing.

Vinaigrette for Swiss Salad:

⅔ cup olive oil	150 ml
⅓ cup red wine vinegar	75 ml
1 tablespoon seasoned salt	15 ml

- Combine all ingredients in bowl and refrigerate. Serves 4.

Stuffed Cucumber Slices

3 cucumbers, peeled
2 (3 ounce) packages cream cheese, softened   **2 (85 g)**
¼ cup stuffed green olives, chopped   **30 g**
½ teaspoon seasoned salt   **2 ml**

- Halve cucumbers lengthwise and scoop out seeds.

- Beat cream cheese in bowl until creamy and add olives
  and seasoned salt. Fill hollows of cucumbers with cream
  cheese mixture.

- Press halves back together, wrap tightly in plastic wrap and
  refrigerate.

- Remove plastic wrap and cut crosswise in ⅓-inch (8 mm) slices
  to serve. Serves 6.

Broccoli-Waldorf Salad

6 cups broccoli florets   **425 g**
1 large red apple with peel, chopped
½ cup golden raisins   **75 g**
½ cup chopped pecans   **55 g**
½ cup coleslaw dressing   **125 ml**

- Combine broccoli, apple, raisins and pecans in large bowl.
  Drizzle with dressing, toss to coat and refrigerate. Serve in pretty
  crystal bowl. Serves 8.

Color-Coded Salad

1 (16 ounce) package tri-colored macaroni, cooked, drained	455 g
1 red bell pepper, cut into julienne strips	
1 cup chopped zucchini	125 g
1 cup broccoli florets	70 g
Caesar salad dressing	

- Combine all ingredients in bowl. Toss with 1 cup (250 ml) salad dressing and refrigerate. Serves 6.

Nutty Cranberry Relish

1 pound fresh cranberries	455 g
2¼ cups sugar	450 g
1 cup orange marmalade	320 g
1 cup chopped pecans, toasted	110 g

- Preheat oven to 350° (175° C).

- Wash and drain cranberries and mix with sugar.

- Place in 1-quart (1 L) baking dish, cover and bake for 1 hour.

- Add marmalade and pecans to cranberry mixture. Mix well, pour into container and refrigerate before serving. Serves 8 to 10.

Broccoli-Chicken Salad

3 - 4 boneless, skinless chicken breast halves,
   cooked, cubed
2 cups fresh broccoli florets   140 g
1 red bell pepper, seeded, chopped
1 cup chopped celery   100 g
Honey-mustard salad dressing

- Combine all ingredients in bowl.

- Toss mixture with honey-mustard salad dressing and refrigerate.
  Serves 6.

Cottage Cheese-Fruit Salad

1 (6 ounce) package orange gelatin   170 g
1 (16 ounce) carton small curd cottage cheese   455 g
2 (11 ounce) cans mandarin oranges, drained   2 (310 g)
1 (20 ounce) can pineapple chunks, drained   570 g
1 (8 ounce) carton whipped topping, thawed   230 g

- Sprinkle gelatin over cottage cheese in bowl and mix well.

- Add oranges and pineapple and mix well. Fold in whipped topping,
  refrigerate and serve in pretty crystal bowl. Serves 12.

Pistachio Salad or Dessert

1 (20 ounce) can crushed pineapple with juice	570 g
1 (3 ounce) package instant pistachio pudding mix	85 g
2 cups miniature marshmallows	90 g
1 cup chopped pecans	110 g
1 (8 ounce) carton whipped topping, thawed	230 g

- Place pineapple in large bowl and sprinkle with pudding mix.

- Add marshmallows and pecans and fold in whipped topping. Pour into crystal serving dish and refrigerate. Serves 12.

Pink Salad

1 (6 ounce) package raspberry gelatin	170 g
1 (20 ounce) can crushed pineapple with juice	570 g
1 cup cream-style cottage cheese	225 g
1 (8 ounce) carton whipped topping, thawed	230 g
¼ cup chopped pecans	30 g

- Place gelatin in large bowl.

- Combine juice from pineapple and, if necessary, enough water to make 1¼ cups (310 ml) liquid in saucepan. Heat, pour over gelatin and mix well.

- Cool in refrigerator just until gelatin begins to thicken. Fold in pineapple, cottage cheese, whipped topping and pecans.

- Pour into molds or 9 x 13-inch (23 x 33 cm) dish and refrigerate. Serves 12.

Cranapple Wiggle

A family friend made this recipe a tradition.

1 (6 ounce) package cherry gelatin	170 g
1 (16 ounce) can whole cranberry sauce	455 g
1 (15 ounce) can crushed pineapple with juice	425 g
1 cup chopped apples	125 g
1 cup chopped pecans	110 g

- Dissolve gelatin in 1½ cups (375 ml) boiling water in bowl and mix well.

- Add cranberry sauce, pineapple, apples and pecans.

- Pour into sprayed 9 x 13-inch (23 x 33 cm) glass dish and refrigerate. Stir about the time it begins to set so the apples will not all stay on top. Serves 12.

Apple-Pineapple Salad

1 (6 ounce) package lemon gelatin	170 g
1 (15 ounce) can pineapple tidbits with juice	425 g
1 cup diced apples with peel	125 g
1 cup chopped pecans	110 g

- Dissolve gelatin in 1 cup (250 ml) boiling water in bowl.

- Add pineapple and place in refrigerator until slightly thick. Fold in apples and pecans.

- Pour into solid mold or 7 x 11-inch (18 x 28 cm) dish and refrigerate until firm. Serves 9.

Frozen Holiday Salad

2 (3 ounce) packages cream cheese, softened	2 (85 g)
3 tablespoons mayonnaise	40 g
¼ cup sugar	50 g
1 (16 ounce) can whole cranberry sauce	455 g
1 (8 ounce) can crushed pineapple, drained	230 g
1 cup chopped pecans	110 g
1 cup miniature marshmallows	45 g
1 (8 ounce) carton whipped topping, thawed	230 g

- Beat cream cheese, mayonnaise and sugar in bowl.

- Add fruit, pecans and marshmallows and fold in whipped topping.

- Pour into sprayed 9 x 13-inch (23 x 33 cm) shallow glass dish and freeze.

- When ready to serve, take salad out of freezer a few minutes before cutting into squares. Serves 12.

If stored in an airtight container, pecans will stay fresh
for 6 months in the pantry or up to a year in the freezer!

Frozen Dessert Salad

1 (8 ounce) package cream cheese, softened	230 g
1 cup powdered sugar	120 g
1 (10 ounce) box frozen strawberries, thawed	280 g
1 (15 ounce) can crushed pineapple, drained	425 g
1 (8 ounce) carton whipped topping, thawed	230 g

- Beat cream cheese and sugar in bowl and fold in strawberries, pineapple and whipped topping. (This will be even better if you stir in ¾ cup (85 g) chopped pecans.)

- Pour into 9 x 9-inch (23 x 23 cm) pan and freeze.

- Cut into squares to serve. Serves 9.

Veggie Salad

Crunchy and good!

5 zucchini, sliced paper thin	
4 yellow squash, sliced paper thin	
1 head cauliflower cut in bite-size pieces	
1 red bell pepper, chopped	
1 bunch green onions with tops, sliced	
2 (2 ounce) packages slivered almonds, toasted	2 (60 g)
1 (8 ounce) bottle creamy Italian salad dressing	250 ml

- Mix zucchini, yellow squash, cauliflower, bell pepper, onions, almonds, ½ teaspoon (2 ml) salt and ¼ teaspoon (1 ml) pepper in bowl. Add dressing and toss. Refrigerate for several hours before serving. Serves 6.

SIDE DISHES

Side Dishes Contents

Cheddar Potatoes

1 (10 ounce) can cheddar cheese soup	280 g
⅓ cup sour cream	80 g
2 green onions with tops, chopped	
3 cups instant seasoned mashed potatoes, prepared	630 g

- Preheat oven to 350° (175° C).

- Heat soup in saucepan and add sour cream, green onions and a little pepper. Stir in potatoes until they blend well.

- Pour into sprayed 2-quart (2 L) baking dish and bake for 25 minutes.

Mashed Potatoes Supreme

1 (8 ounce) package cream cheese, softened	230 g
½ cup sour cream	120 g
2 tablespoons butter, softened	30 g
1 (1 ounce) packet ranch-style salad dressing	30 g
6 - 8 cups warm instant mashed potatoes, prepared	1.3 - 1.7 kg

- Preheat oven to 350° (175° C).

- Combine cream cheese, sour cream, butter and dressing mix in bowl and beat well. Add potatoes and stir well.

- Transfer to 2-quart (2 L) baking dish and bake for 25 minutes or until hot throughout. Serves 4 to 6.

Potatoes Supreme

1 (32 ounce) package frozen hash-brown potatoes, thawed	910 g
1 onion, chopped	
2 (10 ounce) cans cream of chicken soup	2 (280 g)
1 (8 ounce) carton sour cream	230 g

- Preheat oven to 350° (175° C).

- Combine all ingredients in large bowl and mix well.

- Pour into sprayed 9 x 13-inch (23 x 33 cm) baking dish.

- Cover and bake for 1 hour. Serves 8 to 10.

TIP: Sprinkle ½ cup (50 g) parmesan or ½ cup (60 g) cheddar cheese on top before the last 5 minutes of baking.

Potatoes au Gratin

1 (8 ounce) package cubed Velveeta® cheese	230 g
1 (16 ounce) carton half-and-half cream	500 ml
1 cup shredded cheddar cheese	115 g
½ cup (1 stick) butter	115 g
1 (32 ounce) package frozen hash-brown potatoes, thawed	910 g

- Preheat oven to 350° (175° C).

- Melt Velveeta® cheese, half-and-half cream, cheddar cheese and butter in double boiler.

- Place hash browns in sprayed 9 x 13-inch (23 x 33 cm) baking dish and pour cheese mixture over potatoes.

- Bake uncovered for 1 hour. Serves 8 to 10.

Oven Fries

5 medium baking potatoes
⅓ cup canola oil   **75 ml**
¾ teaspoon seasoned salt   **4 ml**
Paprika

- Preheat oven to 375° (190° C).

- Scrub potatoes, cut each in 6 lengthwise wedges and place in shallow baking dish.

- Combine oil, ¼ teaspoon (1 ml) pepper and seasoned salt in bowl and brush potatoes with mixture. Sprinkle potatoes lightly with paprika.

- Bake for about 50 minutes or until potatoes are tender and light brown. Baste twice with remaining oil mixture while baking. Serves 4 to 6.

Twice-Baked Potatoes

8 medium baking potatoes
2 tablespoons butter   **30 g**
1 (10 ounce) can cheddar cheese soup   **280 g**
1 tablespoon dried chives   **15 ml**
Paprika

- Preheat oven to 350° (175° C).

- Bake potatoes for 1 hour or until done.

- Cut potatoes in half lengthwise and scoop flesh from potatoes and leave thin shell.

- Whip potatoes with butter and ½ teaspoon (2 ml) salt in bowl.

- Gradually add soup and chives and beat until light and fluffy.

- Spoon mixture into potato skin shells and sprinkle with paprika.

- Bake at 425° (220° C) for 15 minutes. Serves 8.

TIP: If you want a little "zip" to these potatoes, add
1 (10 ounce/280 g) can fiesta nacho cheese soup instead
of cheddar cheese soup.

Scalloped Potatoes

6 medium potatoes	
½ cup (1 stick) butter	**115 g**
1 tablespoon flour	**15 ml**
2 cups shredded cheddar cheese	**230 g**
¾ cup milk	**175 ml**

- Preheat oven to 350° (175° C).

- Peel and slice potatoes.

- Place half potatoes in sprayed 3-quart (3 L) baking dish. Slice half butter over potatoes, sprinkle with half flour and cover with half cheese.

- Repeat layers with cheese on top. Pour milk over casserole and sprinkle with a little pepper. (Prepare as fast as you can so potatoes will not turn dark. It is a good idea to have all ingredients measured and ready before peeling and slicing potatoes.)

- Cover and bake for 1 hour. Serves 6 to 8.

Sweet Potatoes and Pecans

2 (17 ounce) cans sweet potatoes, drained, divided	**2 (480 g)**
1½ cups packed brown sugar	**330 g**
¼ cup (½ stick) butter, melted	**60 g**
1 cup chopped pecans	**110 g**

- Preheat oven to 350° (175° C).

- Slice half sweet potatoes and place in sprayed 2-quart (2 L) baking dish.

- Combine brown sugar, butter and pecans in bowl and sprinkle half mixture over sweet potatoes.

- Repeat layers and bake uncovered for 30 minutes. Serves 4 to 6.

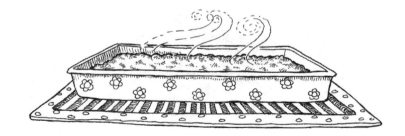

Pasta with Basil

2½ cups small tube pasta	**265 g**
1 small onion, chopped	
2 tablespoons canola oil	**30 ml**
2½ tablespoons dried basil	**37 ml**
1 cup shredded mozzarella cheese	**115 g**

- Cook pasta according to package directions.

- Saute onion in oil in skillet.

- Stir in basil, 1 teaspoon (5 ml) salt and ¼ teaspoon (1 ml) pepper, cook and stir 1 minute.

- Drain pasta and add to basil mixture. (Leave about ½ cup (125 ml) water so pasta won't be too dry.)

- Remove from heat and stir in cheese just until it begins to melt.

- Serve immediately. Serves 8.

Macaroni and Cheese

1 cup macaroni	105 g
1½ cups small curd cottage cheese	340 g
1½ cup shredded cheddar or American cheese	170 g
¼ cup grated parmesan cheese	25 g

- Preheat oven to 350° (175° C).

- Cook macaroni according to package directions and drain. Combine all cheeses and add macaroni to cheese mixture. Spoon into sprayed 2-quart (2 L) baking dish.

- Cover and bake for 35 minutes. Serves 4.

Baked Rice

2 cups rice	370 g
½ cup (1 stick) butter, melted	115 g
1 (10 ounce) can cream of celery soup	280 g
1 (10 ounce) can cream of onion soup	280 g

- Preheat oven to 350° (175° C).

- Combine all ingredients plus 1½ cups (375 ml) water in bowl and mix well.

- Pour into sprayed 3-quart (3 L) baking dish.

- Cover and bake for 1 hour. Serves 6 to 8.

Green Chile-Rice

1 cup cooked instant rice	165 g
1 (12 ounce) package shredded Monterey Jack cheese	340 g
1 (7 ounce) can diced green chilies	200 g
2 (8 ounce) cartons sour cream	2 (230 g)
½ teaspoon garlic powder	2 ml

- Preheat oven to 350° (175° C).

- Combine and mix all ingredients in bowl and add a little salt, if you like.

- Spoon into sprayed 9 x 13-inch (23 x 33 cm) baking dish and bake for 30 minutes. Serves 8 to 10.

Buttered Vegetables

½ cup (1 stick) butter	115 g
2 yellow squash, sliced	
1 (16 ounce) package broccoli florets	455 g
1 (10 ounce) box frozen corn	280 g

- Melt butter in large skillet and add all vegetables.

- Saute vegetables for 10 to 15 minutes or until tender-crisp. Add a little salt if you like and serve warm. Serves 8.

Roasted Vegetables

1½ pounds assorted fresh vegetables	680 g
1 (11 ounce) can sliced water chestnuts, drained	310 g
1 (1 ounce) savory herb with garlic soup mix	30 g
2 tablespoons butter, melted	30 g

- Preheat oven to 400° (205° C).

- Cut all vegetables in uniform 2-inch (5 cm) pieces and place in sprayed 2-quart (2 L) baking dish with water chestnuts.

- Combine melted butter and soup mix in bowl, drizzle mixture over vegetables and stir well.

- Cover and bake for 20 to 25 minutes or until tender and stir once.

- Use your favorite vegetables such as squash, carrots, red bell pepper, zucchini, cauliflower and/or broccoli. Serves 4 to 6.

Shoe-Peg Corn Casserole

½ cup (1 stick) butter	115 g
1 (8 ounce) package cream cheese	230 g
3 (16 ounce) cans shoe-peg corn, drained	3 (455 g)
1 (4 ounce) can diced green chilies	115 g
1½ cups cracker crumbs	90 g

- Preheat oven to 350° (175° C).

- Melt butter in saucepan, stir in cream cheese and mix until cream cheese melts.

- Add corn and green chilies (and some salt and pepper, if you like), mix and pour into sprayed baking dish.

- Sprinkle cracker crumbs over casserole and bake for 25 minutes. Serves 6 to 8.

Fantastic Fried Corn

2 (16 ounce) packages frozen whole kernel corn	2 (455 g)
½ cup (1 stick) butter	115 g
1 cup whipping cream	250 ml
1 tablespoon sugar	15 ml

- Place corn in large skillet over medium heat and add butter, whipping cream, sugar and 1 teaspoon (5 ml) salt.

- Stir constantly and heat until most of whipping cream and butter absorbs into corn. Serves 4 to 6.

Tasty Black-Eyed Peas

2 (10 ounce) packages frozen black-eyed peas	2 (280 g)
1¼ cups chopped green bell pepper	185 g
¾ cup chopped onion	120 g
3 tablespoons butter	45 g
1 (15 ounce) can stewed tomatoes with liquid	425 g

- Cook black-eyed peas according to package directions and drain.

- Saute bell pepper and onion in butter in skillet. Add peas, tomatoes, and a little salt and pepper. Cook over low heat until thoroughly hot and stir often. Serves 4 to 6.

Creamed Green Peas

1 (16 ounce) package frozen green peas	455 g
2 tablespoons butter	30 g
1 (10 ounce) can cream of celery soup	280 g
1 (3 ounce) package cream cheese	85 g
1 (8 ounce) can sliced water chestnuts, drained	230 g

- Cook peas in microwave for 8 minutes and turn dish after 4 minutes.

- Combine butter, soup and cream cheese in large saucepan, cook on medium heat and stir until butter and cream cheese melt.

- Add peas and water chestnuts and mix. Serve hot. Serves 4 to 6.

Baked Onions

4 large onions, thinly sliced
1½ cups crushed potato chips   **85 g**
1 cup shredded cheddar cheese   **115 g**
1 (10 ounce) can cream of chicken soup   **280 g**
¼ cup milk   **60 ml**

- Preheat oven to 300° (150° C).

- Alternate layers of onion, potato chips and cheese in sprayed 9 x 13-inch (23 x 33 cm) baking dish.

- Spoon soup over last layer and pour milk or water over top.

- Sprinkle with a little red or black pepper and bake for 1 hour. Serves 8 to 10.

Creamy Cabbage Bake

1 head cabbage, shredded
1 (10 ounce) can cream of celery soup   **280 g**
⅔ cup milk   **150 ml**
1 (8 ounce) package shredded cheddar cheese   **230 g**

- Preheat oven to 325° (165° C).

- Place cabbage in sprayed 2-quart (2 L) baking dish.

- Dilute celery soup with milk and pour over cabbage.

- Cover and bake for 30 minutes. Uncover, sprinkle with cheese and bake for additional 5 minutes. Serves 4 to 6.

Brown Sugar Carrots

2 (15 ounce) cans sliced carrots	2 (425 g)
¼ cup (½ stick) butter	60 g
3 tablespoons brown sugar	40 g
1 teaspoon ground ginger	5 ml

- Drain carrots and set aside 2 tablespoons (30 ml) liquid.

- Combine reserved liquid with butter, brown sugar and ginger in saucepan and heat thoroughly.

- Add carrots, stir gently and cook for 3 minutes. Serve hot. Serves 4 to 6.

Pine Nut Green Beans

1 (16 ounce) package frozen green beans	455 g
¼ cup (½ stick) butter	60 g
¾ cup pine nuts	95 g
¼ teaspoon garlic powder	1 ml

- Cook beans in water in covered 3-quart (3 L) saucepan for 10 to 15 minutes or until tender-crisp and drain.

- Melt butter in skillet over medium heat, add pine nuts and garlic powder and cook, stirring frequently, until golden.

- Add pine nuts to green beans and sprinkle with a little salt and pepper. Serve hot. Serves 6 to 8.

Parmesan Broccoli

1 (16 ounce) package frozen broccoli spears	**455 g**
½ teaspoon garlic powder	**2 ml**
½ cup breadcrumbs	**60 g**
¼ cup (½ stick) butter, melted	**60 g**
½ cup grated parmesan cheese	**50 g**

- Cook broccoli according to package directions and drain.

- Add garlic powder, breadcrumbs, butter and cheese (and some salt, if you like) and toss. Heat and serve. Serves 4 to 6.

Crunchy Broccoli

2 (10 ounce) packages frozen broccoli florets	**2 (280 g)**
1 (8 ounce) can sliced water chestnuts, drained, chopped	**230 g**
½ cup (1 stick) butter, melted	**115 g**
1 (1 ounce) packet onion soup mix	**30 g**

- Place broccoli in microwave-safe dish, cover and microwave for 5 minutes.

- Turn dish and cook for additional 4 minutes.

- Add water chestnuts.

- Combine melted butter and soup mix in bowl, blend well and toss with broccoli. Serves 4 to 6.

Broccoli-Stuffed Tomatoes

4 medium tomatoes	
1 (10 ounce) package frozen chopped broccoli	**280 g**
1 (6 ounce) roll garlic cheese, softened	**170 g**
½ teaspoon garlic salt	**2 ml**

- Preheat oven to 375° (190° C).

- Cut tops off tomatoes and scoop out flesh.

- Cook broccoli according to package directions and drain well. Combine broccoli, cheese and garlic salt in saucepan and heat just until cheese melts.

- Stuff broccoli mixture into tomatoes and place on baking sheet. Bake for about 10 minutes. Serves 4.

Baked Tomatoes

2 (14 ounce) cans diced tomatoes, drained	**2 (395 g)**
1½ cups breadcrumbs, toasted, divided	**180 g**
Scant ¼ cup sugar	**50 g**
½ onion, chopped	
¼ cup (½ stick) butter, melted	**60 g**

- Preheat oven to 325° (165° C).

- Combine tomatoes, 1 cup (120 g) breadcrumbs, sugar, onion and butter in bowl. Pour into sprayed baking dish and cover with remaining breadcrumbs.

- Bake for 25 to 30 minutes or until crumbs are light brown. Serves 4 to 6.

Baked Eggplant

1 medium eggplant	
¼ cup (½ stick) butter, melted	60 g
1 (5 ounce) can evaporated milk	150 ml
1½ cups cracker crumbs	90 g

- Preheat oven to 350° (175° C).

- Peel, slice and boil eggplant in saucepan until easily mashed and drain.

- Season with a little salt and pepper and add butter, evaporated milk and crumbs.

- Pour into sprayed 2-quart (2 L) baking dish and bake for 25 minutes. Serves 4 to 6.

Fried Zucchini

3 large zucchini, grated	
5 eggs	
1 tube round, buttery crackers, crushed	115 g
½ cup grated parmesan cheese	50 g

- Combine zucchini, eggs and cracker crumbs in bowl and mix well. Add cheese and a little salt and pepper.

- Drop spoonfuls of mixture into skillet with a little oil. Fry for 15 minutes and brown on each side. Serves 4 to 6.

TIP: *One tube round buttery crackers is one-third of 1 (12 ounce/340 g) box.*

Chile-Cheese Squash

1 pound yellow squash	455 g
⅔ cup mayonnaise	150 g
1 (4 ounce) can diced green chilies, drained	115 g
⅔ cup shredded longhorn cheese	75 g
⅔ cup breadcrumbs	80 g

- Cook squash in salted water in saucepan just until tender-crisp and drain.

- Return squash to saucepan and stir in mayonnaise, green chilies, cheese and breadcrumbs. Serve hot. Serves 4 to 6.

Baked Squash

5 cups cooked squash, drained	900 g
¾ cup shredded Monterey Jack cheese	85 g
1 (10 ounce) can cream of chicken soup	280 g
1 (6 ounce) box herb dressing mix	170 g

- Preheat oven to 375° (190° C).

- Place cooked squash in bowl and season with a little salt. Add cheese and soup and blend well.

- Mix dressing according to package directions and place half dressing in sprayed 9 x 13-inch (23 x 33 cm) baking dish.

- Spoon in squash mixture and sprinkle remaining dressing on top. Bake uncovered for 30 minutes. Serves 8 to 10.

Stuffed Yellow Squash

5 large yellow squash	
1 (16 ounce) package frozen chopped spinach	455 g
1 (8 ounce) package cream cheese, cubed	230 g
1 (1 ounce) packet onion soup mix	30 g
Shredded cheddar cheese	

- Preheat oven to 325° (165° C).

- Steam whole squash until tender. Cut squash lengthwise and remove seeds with spoon.

- Cook spinach according to package directions and drain well. Add cream cheese to cooked spinach and stir until it melts. (Do not let it boil.)

- Add soup mix and blend well. Fill scooped out squash shells with spinach mixture and top with few sprinkles cheese. Place on baking sheet and bake for 15 minutes. Serves 6 to 8.

Zucchini Bake

4 cups grated zucchini	500 g
1½ cups shredded Monterey Jack cheese	170 g
4 eggs, beaten	
2 cups cheese cracker crumbs	120 g

- Preheat oven to 350° (175° C).

- Combine zucchini, cheese and eggs in bowl and mix well. Spoon into sprayed 3-quart (3 L) baking dish and sprinkle cracker crumbs over top. Bake uncovered for 35 minutes. Serves 6 to 8.

Creamed-Spinach Bake

2 (10 ounce) packages frozen chopped spinach	2 (280 g)
2 (3 ounce) packages cream cheese, softened	2 (85 g)
3 tablespoons butter	45 g
1 cup seasoned breadcrumbs	120 g

- Preheat oven to 350° (175° C).

- Cook spinach according to package directions and drain.

- Combine cream cheese and butter with spinach and heat until they melt and mix well with spinach. Pour into sprayed 2-quart (2L) baking dish and sprinkle a little salt over spinach.

- Cover with breadcrumbs and bake for 15 to 20 minutes. Serves 4 to 6.

Spinach Casserole

1 (16 ounce) package frozen chopped spinach	455 g
1 (8 ounce) package cream cheese and chives	230 g
1 (10 ounce) can cream of mushroom soup	280 g
1 egg, beaten	
Cracker crumbs	

- Preheat oven to 350° (175° C).

- Cook spinach according to package directions and drain.

- Blend cream cheese and soup with egg in bowl, mix with spinach and pour into 2-quart (2L) sprayed baking dish. Top with cracker crumbs and bake for 35 minutes. Serves 4 to 6.

Baked Beans

2 (15 ounce) cans pork and beans, slightly drained	**2 (425 g)**
½ onion, finely chopped	
⅔ cup packed brown sugar	**145 g**
¼ cup chili sauce	**30 g**
1 tablespoon Worcestershire sauce	**15 ml**
2 strips bacon	

- Preheat oven to 325° (165° C).

- Combine beans, onion, brown sugar, chili sauce and Worcestershire in bowl. Pour into sprayed 2-quart (2 L) baking dish and place bacon strips over bean mixture.

- Bake uncovered for 50 minutes. Serves 4 to 6.

Savory Cauliflower

1 head cauliflower	
1 (1 ounce) package hollandaise sauce mix	**30 g**
Fresh parsley	
Lemon slices, optional	

- Cut cauliflower into small florets and cook in salted water until barely tender. (Be VERY careful not to overcook cauliflower.)

- Mix sauce according to package directions.

- Drain cauliflower, top with sauce and sprinkle with parsley. Garnish with lemon slices, if you like. Serves 4 to 6.

Cauliflower Medley

1 head cauliflower, cut into florets	
1 (14 ounce) can Italian stewed tomatoes with juice	**395 g**
1 bell pepper, seeded, chopped	
1 onion, chopped	
¼ cup (½ stick) butter	**60 g**
1 cup shredded cheddar cheese	**115 g**

- Preheat oven to 350° (175° C).

- Combine cauliflower, stewed tomatoes, bell pepper, onion and butter in large saucepan with about 2 tablespoons (30 ml) water and a little salt and pepper.

- Cover and cook until cauliflower is done, about 10 to 15 minutes. (Do not let cauliflower get mushy.)

- Place in 2-quart (2 L) baking dish and sprinkle cheese on top.

- Bake just until cheese melts. Serves 4 to 6.

Asparagus Bake

4 (10 ounce) cans asparagus	4 (280 g)
3 eggs, hard-boiled, sliced	
⅓ cup milk	75 ml
1½ cups shredded cheddar cheese	170 g
1¼ cups cheese cracker crumbs	75 g

- Preheat oven to 350° (175° C).

- Place asparagus in sprayed 7 x 11-inch (18 x 28 cm) baking dish, layer hard-boiled eggs on top and pour milk over casserole.

- Sprinkle cheese on top and add cracker crumbs.

- Bake uncovered for 30 minutes. Serves 6 to 8.

Sesame Asparagus

6 fresh asparagus spears, trimmed	
1 tablespoon butter	15 ml
1 teaspoon lemon juice	5 ml
1 teaspoon sesame seeds	5 ml

- Place asparagus in skillet (sprinkle with salt if desired), add ¼ cup (60 ml) water and bring to a boil. Reduce heat, cover and simmer for 4 minutes.

- Melt butter in saucepan and add lemon juice and sesame seeds.

- Drain asparagus and drizzle with butter mixture. Serves 4.

Creamy Vegetable Casserole

1 (16 ounce) package frozen broccoli, carrots and cauliflower	455 g
1 (10 ounce) can cream of mushroom soup	280 g
1 (8 ounce) carton garden vegetable cream cheese	230 g
1 cup seasoned croutons	40 g

- Preheat oven to 375° (190° C).

- Cook vegetables according to package directions, drain and place in large bowl.

- Heat soup and cream cheese in saucepan just enough to mix easily.

- Pour soup mixture into vegetable mixture, stir well and pour into 2-quart (2 L) baking dish.

- Sprinkle with croutons and bake uncovered for 25 minutes or until bubbly. Serves 4 to 6.

Corn Vegetable Medley

1 (10 ounce) can golden corn soup	**280 g**
½ cup milk	**125 ml**
2 cups broccoli florets	**140 g**
2 cups cauliflower florets	**200 g**
1 cup shredded cheddar cheese	**115 g**

- Heat soup and milk in saucepan over medium heat to boiling and stir often.

- Stir in broccoli and cauliflower florets and return to boiling.

- Reduce heat to low and cover. Cook for 20 minutes or until vegetables are tender and stir occasionally.

- Stir in cheese and heat until cheese melts. Serves 4 to 6.

Calico Corn

1 (16 ounce) package frozen whole kernel corn	**455 g**
1 bell pepper, chopped	
⅓ cup chopped celery	**35 g**
1 (10 ounce) can cheddar cheese soup	**280 g**

- Preheat oven to 350° (175° C).

- Cook corn in microwave according to package directions and drain well. Add bell pepper and celery. Stir in soup and mix well.

- Pour into sprayed 2-quart (2 L) baking dish. Cover and bake for 30 minutes. Serves 4 to 6.

BEEF
MAIN DISHES

Beef Main Dishes Contents

The best way to avoid freezer burn is to wrap food twice in plastic wrap and seal in an air-tight plastic bag. Be sure to use a permanent marker to date and label your package.

Cheesy Beefy Gnocchi

1 pound lean ground beef	455 g
1 (10 ounce) can cheddar cheese soup	280 g
1 (10 ounce) can tomato bisque soup	280 g
2 cups gnocchi or shell pasta	210 g

- Cook beef in skillet until brown and drain.

- Add soups, pasta and 1½ cups (375 ml) water and bring mixture to a boil.

- Cover and cook over medium heat for 10 to 12 minutes or until pasta is done. Stir often. Serves 8.

Chili Casserole

1 (40 ounce) can chili with beans	1.1 kg
2 (4 ounce) cans diced green chilies	2 (115 g)
1 (2 ounce) can sliced ripe olives, drained	60 g
1 (8 ounce) package shredded cheddar cheese	230 g
2 cups crushed ranch-flavored tortilla chips	175 g

- Preheat oven to 350° (175° C).

- Combine all ingredients in bowl and transfer to sprayed 3-quart (3 L) baking dish.

- Bake uncovered for 35 minutes or until bubbly. Serves 6.

Potato-Beef Casserole

4 medium potatoes, peeled, sliced	
1¼ pounds lean ground beef, browned, drained	570 g
1 (10 ounce) can cream of mushroom soup	280 g
1 (10 ounce) can vegetable beef soup	280 g

- Preheat oven to 350° (175° C).

- Combine all ingredients plus ½ teaspoon each of salt and pepper in bowl and transfer to sprayed 3-quart (3 L) baking dish.

- Cover and bake for 1 hour 30 minutes or until potatoes are tender. Serves 6.

Casserole Supper

1 (1 pound) lean ground beef	455 g
¼ cup rice	45 g
1 (10 ounce) can French onion soup	280 g
1 (3 ounce) can french-fried onions	85 g

- Preheat oven to 325° (165° C).

- Brown ground beef in skillet, drain and place in sprayed 7 x 11-inch (18 x 28 cm) baking dish. Add rice, onion soup and ½ cup (125 ml) water.

- Cover and bake for 40 minutes. Uncover, sprinkle onions over top and bake for 10 minutes. Serves 4 to 6.

Steak-Bake Italiano

2 pounds lean round steak	910 g
2 teaspoons Italian herb seasoning	10 ml
1 teaspoon garlic salt	5 ml
2 (15 ounce) cans stewed tomatoes	2 (425 g)

- Preheat oven to 325° (165° C).

- Cut steak into serving-size pieces, brown in skillet and place in 9 x 13-inch (23 x 33 cm) baking dish.

- Combine herb seasoning, garlic salt and stewed tomatoes in bowl, mix well and pour over steak pieces.

- Cover and bake for 1 hour. Serves 6 to 8.

Easy Chili

2 pounds lean ground beef	910 g
1 onion, chopped	
4 (16 ounce) cans chili-hot beans with liquid	4 (455 g)
1 (1 ounce) package chili seasoning mix	30 g
1 (46 ounce) can tomato juice	1.4 L

- Cook beef and onion in large, heavy pan, stir until meat crumbles and drain.

- Stir in remaining ingredients. Bring mixture to a boil, reduce heat and simmer, and stir occasionally, for 2 hours. Serves 6.

Taco Pie

1½ pounds lean ground beef	680 g
½ green bell pepper, chopped	
1 teaspoon canola oil	5 ml
1 (15 ounce) can Mexican stewed tomatoes	425 g
1 tablespoon chili powder	15 ml
¼ teaspoon garlic powder	1 ml
1½ cups shredded cheddar cheese	170 g
1 (6 ounce) package corn muffin mix	170 g
1 egg	
⅔ cup milk	150 ml

- Preheat oven to 375° (190° C).

- Brown ground beef and bell pepper in large skillet in oil and drain well.

- Add ½ teaspoon (5 ml) salt, tomatoes, 1 cup (250 ml) water, chili powder and garlic powder. Cook on medium heat for about 10 minutes or until most of liquid is gone.

- Pour into sprayed 9 x 13-inch (23 x 33 cm) baking dish. Sprinkle cheese on top.

- Combine corn muffin mix, egg and milk in bowl and beat well. Pour over cheese.

- Bake for 25 minutes or until corn muffin mix is light brown.

- Remove from oven and let stand for about 10 minutes before serving. Serves 6 to 8.

Simple Spaghetti Bake

8 ounces spaghetti	230 g
1 (1 pound) lean ground beef	455 g
1 green bell pepper, finely chopped	
1 onion, chopped	
1 (10 ounce) can tomato bisque soup	280 g
1 (15 ounce) can tomato sauce	425 g
2 teaspoons Italian seasoning	10 ml
1 (8 ounce) can whole kernel corn, drained	230 g
1 (4 ounce) can sliced black olives, drained	115 g
1 (12 ounce) package shredded cheddar cheese	340 g

- Cook spaghetti according to package directions, drain and set aside.

- Cook beef, bell pepper and onion in skillet and drain.

- Add remaining ingredients, ⅓ cup (75 ml) water and ½ teaspoon (2 ml) salt and spaghetti to beef mixture and stir well. Pour into sprayed 9 x 13-inch (23 x 33 cm) baking dish and cover. Refrigerate for 2 to 3 hours.

- When ready to bake, preheat oven to 350° (175° C).

- Cover and bake for 45 minutes. Serves 6 to 8.

Easy Winter Warmer

This is such a good spaghetti sauce on noodles and is a great substitute for cream sauce.

1 (12 ounce) package medium egg noodles	340 g
Canola oil	
3 tablespoons butter	45 g
1½ pounds lean ground round beef	680 g
1 (10 ounce) package frozen seasoning blend (chopped onions and peppers), thawed	280 g
1 (28 ounce) jar spaghetti sauce, divided	795 g
1 (12 ounce) package shredded mozzarella cheese, divided	340 g

- Preheat oven to 350° (175° C).

- Cook noodles according to package directions in pot of boiling water with a dab of oil and salt. Drain thoroughly, add butter and stir until butter melts.

- Brown beef and onions and peppers in skillet and drain thoroughly.

- Pour half of spaghetti sauce in sprayed 9 x 13-inch (23 x 33 cm) baking dish.

- Layer half noodles, half beef and half cheese. Repeat for second layer. Cover and bake for about 30 minutes or until dish is hot. Serves 6 to 8.

Pepper Steak

1 (1¼ pound) sirloin steak, cut in strips	570 g
Seasoned salt	
1 (16 ounce) package frozen bell pepper and onion strips, thawed	455 g
1 (16 ounce) package cubed Mexican Velveeta® cheese	455 g
Rice, cooked	

- Sprinkle steak with seasoned salt.

- Cook steak strips in sprayed large skillet for 10 minutes or until no longer pink.

- Remove steak from skillet and set aside.

- Stir in vegetables and ½ cup (125 ml) water and simmer vegetables for 5 minutes or until all liquid cooks out.

- Add cheese and turn heat to medium-low.

- When cheese melts, stir in steak and serve over rice. Serves 4.

Ravioli and More

1 (1 pound) lean ground beef	455 g
1 teaspoon garlic powder	5 ml
1 large onion, chopped	
2 zucchini, grated	
¼ cup (½ stick) butter	60 g
1 (28 ounce) jar spaghetti sauce	795 g
1 (25 ounce) package cooked ravioli with portobello mushrooms	710 g
1 (12 ounce) package shredded mozzarella cheese	340 g

- Preheat oven to 350° (175° C).

- Brown ground beef in large skillet until no longer pink and drain. Add garlic powder and ½ teaspoon (2 ml) salt.

- Cook onion and zucchini in butter in saucepan just until tender-crisp and stir in spaghetti sauce.

- Spread ½ cup (125 ml) sauce in sprayed 9 x 13-inch (23 x 33 cm) baking dish. Layer half ravioli, half spaghetti sauce, half beef and half cheese. Repeat layers, but omit remaining cheese. Cover and bake for 35 minutes.

- Uncover and sprinkle remaining cheese. Let stand for 10 minutes before serving. Serves 6 to 8.

Asian Beef and Noodles

1¼ pounds ground beef	570 g
1 (16 ounce) package frozen oriental stir-fry vegetable mixture	455 g
2 (3 ounce) packages Oriental-flavored ramen noodles	2 (85 g)
½ teaspoon ground ginger	2 ml
3 tablespoons thinly sliced green onions	20 g

- Brown ground beef in large skillet and drain.

- Add ½ cup (125 ml) water and a little salt and pepper, simmer for 10 minutes and transfer to separate bowl.

- In same skillet, combine 2 cups (500 ml) water, vegetables, noodles (broken up), both seasoning packets and ginger.

- Bring to a boil and reduce heat.

- Cover and simmer for 3 minutes or until noodles are tender, stir occasionally.

- Return beef to skillet and stir in green onions. Serve right from skillet. Serves 6.

Pinto Beef Pie

1 (1 pound) lean ground beef	455 g
1 onion, chopped	
2 (16 ounce) cans pinto beans with liquid, divided	2 (455 g)
1 (10 ounce) can tomatoes and green chilies with liquid, divided	280 g
1 (6 ounce) can french-fried onions	170 g

- Preheat oven to 350° (175° C).

- Brown beef and onion in skillet and drain.

- Layer 1 can beans, half beef-onion mixture and ½ can tomatoes and green chilies in sprayed 2-quart (2 L) baking dish. Repeat layers.

- Top with onions and bake uncovered for 30 minutes. Serves 4.

Smothered Beef Patties

1½ pounds ground beef	680 g
½ cup chili sauce	135 g
½ cup round, buttery cracker crumbs	30 g
1 (14 ounce) can beef broth	395 g

- Combine beef, chili sauce and cracker crumbs in bowl and form into 5 or 6 patties. Brown patties in skillet, pour beef broth over patties and bring to a boil. Reduce heat, cover and simmer for 40 minutes. Serves 5 to 6.

Shepherds' Pie

1 pound lean ground beef	455 g
1 (1 ounce) packet taco seasoning mix	30 g
1 cup shredded cheddar cheese	115 g
1 (11 ounce) can whole kernel corn, drained	310 g
2 cups instant mashed potatoes, prepared	420 g

- Preheat oven to 350° (175° C).

- Brown beef in skillet, cook for 10 minutes and drain.

- Add taco seasoning and ¾ cup (175 ml) water and cook for additional 5 minutes. Spoon beef mixture into 8-inch (20 cm) baking pan and sprinkle cheese on top.

- Sprinkle with corn and spread mashed potatoes over top. Bake for 25 minutes or until top is golden. Serves 4 to 6.

Spanish Meatloaf

1½ pounds lean ground beef	680 g
1 (16 ounce) can Spanish rice	455 g
1 egg, beaten	
¾ cup round, buttery cracker crumbs	45 g
Chunky salsa	

- Preheat oven to 350° (175° C). Combine beef, rice, egg and cracker crumbs in bowl and shape into sprayed loaf pan. Bake for 1 hour. Serve topped with salsa. Serves 6 to 8.

Potato-Beef Bake

This is really good sprinkled with
1 cup (115 g) shredded cheddar cheese.

1 pound ground beef	**455 g**
1 (10 ounce) can sloppy Joe sauce	**280 g**
1 (10 ounce) can fiesta nacho cheese soup	**280 g**
1 (32 ounce) package frozen hash-brown potatoes, thawed	**910 g**

- Preheat oven to 400° (205° C).

- Cook beef in skillet over medium heat until no longer pink and drain.

- Add sloppy Joe sauce and cheese soup to beef and mix well.

- Place hash browns in sprayed 9 x 13-inch (23 x 33 cm) baking dish and top with beef mixture.

- Cover and bake for 25 minutes.

- Uncover and bake for additional 10 minutes. Serves 6 to 8.

Delicious Meatloaf

1½ pounds lean ground beef	680 g
⅔ cup Italian-seasoned breadcrumbs	80 g
1 (10 ounce) can golden mushroom soup, divided	280 g
2 eggs, beaten	
2 tablespoons butter	30 g

- Preheat oven to 350° (175° C).

- Mix beef, breadcrumbs, half mushroom soup and eggs in bowl thoroughly.   Shape firmly into 8 x 4-inch (20 x 10 cm) loaf pan and bake for 45 minutes.

- Mix butter, remaining soup and ¼ cup (60 ml) water in small saucepan, heat thoroughly and serve sauce over meatloaf. Serves 6 to 8.

Slow Cookin', Good Tastin' Brisket

½ cup hickory-flavored liquid smoke	125 ml
1 (4 - 5 pound) beef brisket	1.8 - 2.3 kg
1 (5 ounce) bottle Worcestershire sauce	150 ml
¾ cup barbecue sauce	200 g

- Preheat oven to 275° (135° C). Pour liquid smoke over brisket, cover and refrigerate overnight.

- Drain; add Worcestershire sauce over brisket. Cover and bake for 6 to 7 hours. Cover with barbecue sauce and bake uncovered for additional 30 minutes. Slice very thinly across grain. Serves 8.

Baked Onion-Mushroom Steak

1½ pounds (½ inch) thick round steak	680 g/1.2 cm
1 (10 ounce) can cream of mushroom soup	280 g
1 (1 ounce) packet onion soup mix	30 g

- Preheat oven to 325° (165° C).

- Place steak in sprayed 9 x 13-inch (23 x 33 cm) baking dish and sprinkle with a little salt and pepper.

- Pour mushroom soup and ½ cup (125 ml) water over steak and sprinkle with onion soup mix.

- Cover and bake for 2 hours. Serves 8.

Smothered Beef Steak

2 pounds lean round steak	910 g
1 cup rice	185 g
1 (14 ounce) can beef broth	395 g
1 green bell pepper, chopped	

- Cut steak into serving-size pieces and brown in very large skillet.

- Add rice, beef broth, bell pepper and 1 cup (250 ml) water to skillet and bring to a boil.

- Reduce heat, cover and simmer for 1 hour. Serves 6 to 8.

Red Wine Round Steak

2 pounds (¾ inch) thick round steak	940 g/1.8 cm
Canola oil	
1 (1 ounce) packet onion soup mix	30 g
1 cup dry red wine	250 ml
1 (4 ounce) can sliced mushrooms	115 g

• Preheat oven to 325° (165° C).

• Remove all fat from steak and cut into serving-size pieces. Brown meat in skillet with a little oil. When browned on both sides, place in sprayed 9 x 13-inch (23 x 33 cm) baking dish.

• Combine soup mix, wine, mushrooms and 1 cup (250 ml) hot water in skillet and pour over steak. Cover and bake for 1 hour 20 minutes or until steak is tender. Serves 6 to 8.

Smothered Steak

1 (2 pound) round steak	910 g
1 (10 ounce) can golden mushroom soup	280 g
1 (1 ounce) packet onion soup mix	30 g
⅔ cup milk	150 ml

• Preheat oven to 325° (165° C). Cut steak into serving-size pieces and place in sprayed 9 x 13-inch (23 x 33 cm) baking pan.

• Combine mushroom soup, soup mix and milk in saucepan. Heat just enough to mix well and pour over steak. Cover and bake for 1 hour. Serves 6 to 8.

Lean Mean Round Steak

Flour	
1 teaspoon paprika	**5 ml**
2 pounds lean round steak, cut into strips	**910 g**
2 tablespoons canola oil	**30 ml**
1 cup chopped onion	**160 g**
½ cup chopped green bell pepper	**75 g**
2 (15 ounce) cans Mexican stewed tomatoes	**2 (425 g)**
2 (8 ounce) cans tomato sauce	**2 (230 g)**
1 tablespoon chili powder	**15 ml**
Shredded cheddar cheese	
Fresh cilantro	
Rice, cooked	

- Combine flour, paprika and a little salt and pepper in bowl. Dredge steak strips in flour and set aside.

- Heat oil in large, heavy skillet over medium heat. Brown meat and add onion, bell pepper, tomatoes, tomato sauce, chili powder and 1 cup (250 ml) water. Reduce heat to medium-low, cover and simmer for 1 hour.

- To serve, arrange steak on hot, ovenproof serving platter and cover with sauce. Sprinkle shredded cheese on top.

- Place under broiler for 1 to 2 minutes or until cheese melts. Garnish with fresh cilantro.

- Serve over rice. Serves 6 to 8.

Roasted Garlic Steak

2 (15 ounce) cans tomato soup with roasted
  garlic and herbs   2 (425 g)
½ cup Italian salad dressing   125 ml
1½ pounds (¾ inch) thick boneless beef
  sirloin steak   680 g/1.8 cm

- Combine soup, salad dressing and ⅓ cup (75 ml) water in saucepan.

- Broil steaks to desired doneness. (Allow 15 minutes for medium.) Turn once and brush often with sauce.

- Heat remaining sauce to serve with steak. Serves 8.

Pot Roast

4 - 6 pound chuck roast   1.8 - 2.7 kg
1 (10 ounce) can French onion soup   280 g
1 (1 ounce) packet onion soup mix   30 g
4 - 6 potatoes, peeled, quartered

- Preheat oven to 350° (175° C).

- Place roast on large sheet of heavy-duty foil.

- Combine soup and soup mix in bowl and spread over roast.

- Add potatoes and secure edges of foil tightly.

- Bake for 3 to 4 hours. Serves 8.

Next-Day Beef

1 (5 - 6 pound) trimmed beef brisket	**2.3 - 2.7 kg**
1 (1 ounce) packet onion soup mix	**30 g**
1 (10 ounce) bottle steak sauce	**280 g**
1 (12 ounce) bottle barbecue sauce	**340 g**

- Preheat oven to 325° (165° C).

- Place brisket, cut-side up in roasting pan.

- Combine onion soup mix, steak and barbecue sauces in bowl and pour over brisket.

- Cover and bake for 4 to 5 hours or until tender.

- Remove brisket from pan, pour off drippings and refrigerate both separately overnight.

- The next day, trim all fat from meat, slice and reheat.

- Skim fat off drippings, reheat and serve sauce over brisket. Serves 8 to 10.

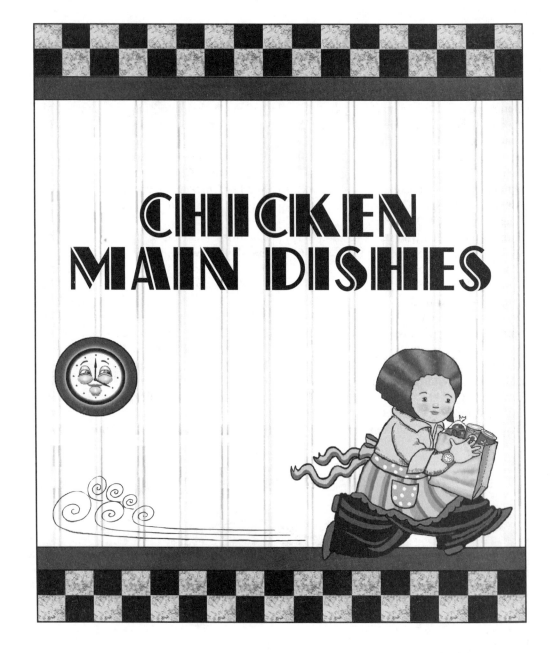

CHICKEN MAIN DISHES

Chicken Main Dishes Contents

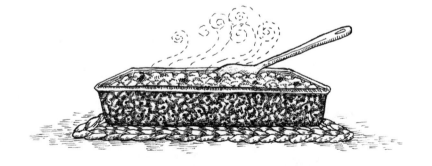

Deluxe Dinner Nachos

Nachos:

1 (14 ounce) package tortilla chips, divided	395 g
1 (8 ounce) package shredded Velveeta® cheese, divided	230 g
1 (8 ounce) can diced jalapenos, divided	230 g

Deluxe Nacho Topping:

1 (11 ounce) can Mexicorn® with liquid	310 g
1 (15 ounce) can jalapeno pinto beans, drained	425 g
2 cups skinned, chopped rotisserie chicken	280 g
1 bunch green onions, chopped	
Salsa	

- Preheat oven to 400° (205° C).

- Place about three-quarters of tortilla chips in sprayed baking dish. Sprinkle half cheese and half jalapenos on top. Bake just until cheese melts.

- Combine corn, beans and chicken in saucepan. Heat over medium heat, stirring until mixture is hot. Spoon mixture over nachos, place dish in oven and bake for about 10 minutes.

- Sprinkle remaining cheese and green onions over top and serve immediately. Garnish with remaining jalapenos, remaining tortillas and salsa. Serves 4 to 6.

Chucky Clucky Casserole

1 (16 ounce) package frozen broccoli spears	455 g
3 cups cooked, diced chicken	420 g
1 (10 ounce) can cream of chicken soup	280 g
2 tablespoons milk	30 ml
⅓ cup mayonnaise	75 g
2 teaspoons lemon juice	10 ml
3 tablespoons butter, melted	45 g
1 cup breadcrumbs or cracker crumbs	120 g
⅓ cup shredded cheddar cheese	40 g

- Preheat oven to 350° (175° C).

- Cook broccoli according to package directions and drain. Place broccoli in sprayed 9 x 13-inch (23 x 33 cm) glass baking dish. Sprinkle 1 teaspoon (5 ml) salt over broccoli and cover with diced chicken.

- Combine soup, milk, mayonnaise, lemon juice and ¼ teaspoon (1 ml) pepper in saucepan. Heat just enough to dilute soup a little and pour over chicken.

- Mix melted butter, breadcrumbs and cheese in bowl and sprinkle over soup mixture. Bake uncovered for 30 minutes or until mixture is hot and bubbly. Serves 6 to 8.

Chicken Chow Mein

3½ cups cooked, cubed chicken breasts	490 g
2 (10 ounce) cans cream of chicken soup	2 (280 g)
2 (15 ounce) cans chop suey vegetables, drained	2 (425 g)
1 (8 ounce) can sliced water chestnuts, drained	230 g
¾ cup chopped cashews	100 g
1 green bell pepper, chopped	
1 onion, chopped	
1 cup chopped celery	100 g
¼ teaspoon hot sauce	1 ml
1¼ cups chow mein noodles	70 g

- Preheat oven to 350° (175° C).

- Combine chicken, soup, vegetables, water chestnuts, cashews, bell pepper, onion, celery and hot sauce in large bowl. Stir to mix well.

- Spoon into sprayed 9 x 13-inch (23 x 33 cm) baking dish. Sprinkle chow mein noodles over top of casserole.

- Bake uncovered for 35 minutes or until it bubbles at edges of casserole. Let stand for 5 minutes before serving. Serves 6 to 8.

Chicken Spaghetti

3 chicken breasts, cooked
1 (10 ounce) can tomatoes and green chilies   280 g
1 (10 ounce) can cream of mushroom soup   280 g
1 (8 ounce) package shredded cheddar cheese   230 g
1 (8 ounce) package shredded Velveeta® cheese   230 g
1 (12 ounce) package spaghetti   340 g

- Preheat oven to 350° (175° C).

- Shred cooked chicken into large bowl. Add tomatoes and green chilies, soup, cheddar cheese and Velveeta® cheese.

- Cook spaghetti according to package directions and drain.

- Add to chicken mixture; mix well. Pour into 3-quart (3 L) baking dish and bake for 35 minutes. Serves 6.

Statistical studies are finding that family meals play a significant role in childhood development. Children who eat with their families four or more nights per week are healthier, make better grades, score higher on aptitude tests, and are less likely to have problems with drugs.

Alfredo Chicken

5 - 6 boneless, skinless chicken breast halves
Canola oil
1 (16 ounce) package frozen broccoli florets, thawed 455 g
1 red bell pepper, seeded, chopped
1 (16 ounce) jar alfredo sauce 455 g

- Preheat oven to 325° (165° C).

- Brown and cook chicken breasts in large skillet with a little oil until juices run clear. Transfer to sprayed 9 x 13-inch (23 x 33 cm) baking dish.

- Microwave broccoli according to package directions and drain. Spoon broccoli and bell pepper over chicken.

- Heat alfredo sauce with ¼ cup (60 ml) water in small saucepan. Pour over chicken and vegetables. Cover and cook for 15 to 20 minutes. Serves 5 to 6.

TIP: This chicken-broccoli dish can be "dressed up" a bit by sprinkling shredded parmesan cheese on top after casserole bakes.

Quickie Russian Chicken

This is great when you don't have time to cook.

6 boneless, skinless chicken breast halves
1 (8 ounce) bottle Russian salad dressing   **250 ml**
1 (5 ounce) jar apricot preserves   **145 g**
1 (1 ounce) packet onion soup mix   **30 g**

- Preheat oven to 350° (175° C).

- Place chicken breasts in sprayed, shallow baking dish.

- Combine dressing, apricot preserves, onion soup mix and ¼ cup (60 ml) water in saucepan and bring to a slow boil. Remove from heat and pour over chicken.

- Cover and bake for 1 hour. Uncover, baste with sauce and bake for additional 30 minutes. Serve immediately. Serves 6.

Aztec Creamy Salsa Chicken

6 boneless, skinless chicken breast halves	
Canola oil	
1 (1 ounce) packet taco seasoning mix	**30 g**
1 (16 ounce) jar salsa	**455 g**
1 (8 ounce) carton sour cream	**230 g**

- Preheat oven to 350° (175° C).

- Brown chicken breasts in oil in skillet and transfer to sprayed 9 x 13-inch (23 x 33 cm) baking dish. Sprinkle taco seasoning over chicken and top with salsa.

- Cover and bake for 35 minutes.

- Remove chicken to serving plates. Add sour cream to juices in pan, stir well and microwave on HIGH for about 2 minutes for sauce to serve over chicken. Serves 6.

Finger Lickin' BBQ Chicken

1 (2 pound) chicken, quartered	910 g
½ cup ketchup	135 g
¼ cup (½ stick) butter, melted	60 g
2 tablespoons sugar	25 g
1 tablespoon mustard	15 ml
½ teaspoon minced garlic	2 ml
¼ cup lemon juice	60 ml
¼ cup white vinegar	60 ml
¼ cup Worcestershire sauce	60 ml

- Preheat oven to 325° (165° C).

- Sprinkle chicken quarters with salt and pepper and brown in skillet. Place in large sprayed baking pan.

- Combine ketchup, butter, sugar, mustard, garlic, lemon juice, vinegar and Worcestershire in bowl. Pour over chicken.

- Cover and bake for 50 minutes. Serves 4 to 6.

An easy way to get seasonings and spices to stick to chicken and roasts is to place them on plastic wrap, season well on all sides and roll meat in plastic wrap. By pressing seasonings into meat, they are more likely to stay on all sides. Remove wrap and cook.

Parmesan Chicken Breasts

6 boneless, skinless chicken breast halves	
1½ cups breadcrumbs	**180 g**
½ cup grated parmesan cheese	**50 g**
1 teaspoon dried basil	**5 ml**
½ teaspoon garlic powder	**2 ml**
1 (8 ounce) carton sour cream	**230 g**

- Preheat oven to 325° (165° C).

- Flatten chicken to ½-inch (1.2 cm) thickness. Combine breadcrumbs, parmesan cheese, basil and garlic powder in shallow dish.

- Dip chicken in sour cream, coat with crumb mixture and place (so chicken breasts do not touch) in sprayed 10 x 15-inch (25 x 38 cm) baking dish.

- Bake uncovered for 50 to 60 minutes or until golden brown. Serves 6.

Chile-Chicken Roll-Ups

8 boneless, skinless chicken breast halves
2 (4 ounce) cans diced green chilies   **2 (115 g)**
1 (8 ounce) package shredded cheddar cheese   **230 g**
½ cup (1 stick) butter, melted   **115 g**
2 cups crushed tortilla chips   **175 g**

- Place each chicken breast on wax paper, flatten to about ¼-inch (.6 cm) thickness with rolling pin or mallet and season with 1 teaspoon (5 ml) salt and ½ teaspoon (2 ml) pepper.

- Place green chilies and a little cheese evenly in center of each chicken breast. Carefully roll each chicken breast so no green chilies or cheese seep out and secure with toothpicks.

- Place chicken breasts in small baking dish and refrigerate for several hours or overnight.

- When ready to bake, preheat oven to 350° (175° C).

- Roll each chicken breast in melted butter and crushed tortilla chips. Bake for about 25 to 30 minutes or until tender. Serves 8.

Chicken Quesadillas

3 boneless, skinless chicken breast halves, cubed
1 (10 ounce) can cheddar cheese soup   **280 g**
⅔ cup chunky salsa   **175 g**
10 flour tortillas

- Preheat oven to 400° (205° C).

- Cook chicken in skillet until juices evaporate and stir often. Add soup and salsa and heat thoroughly.

- Spread about ⅓ cup (75 ml) soup mixture on half tortilla to within ½ inch (1.2 cm) of edge. Moisten edge with water, fold over and seal. Place tortillas on 2 baking sheets. Bake for 5 to 6 minutes. Serves 5.

Cola Chicken

4 - 6 boneless, skinless chicken breast halves
1 cup ketchup   **170 g**
1 cup cola   **250 ml**
2 tablespoons Worcestershire sauce   **30 ml**

- Preheat oven to 350° (175° C).

- Place chicken in 9 x 13-inch (23 x 33 cm) baking dish and sprinkle with salt and pepper.

- Mix ketchup, cola and Worcestershire sauce in bowl and pour over chicken. Cover and bake for 50 minutes. Serves 4 to 6.

Crunchy Chip Chicken

1½ cups crushed sour cream potato chips	85 g
1 tablespoon dried parsley	15 ml
1 egg, beaten	
1 tablespoon Worcestershire sauce	15 ml
4 large boneless, skinless chicken breast halves	
¼ cup canola oil	60 ml

- Combine potato chips and parsley in shallow bowl.

- In separate shallow bowl, combine beaten egg, Worcestershire and 1 tablespoon (15 ml) water.

- Dip chicken pieces in egg mixture and dredge chicken in potato chip mixture. Heat oil in heavy skillet and fry chicken pieces in skillet for about 10 minutes.

- Turn each piece over and cook for additional 10 minutes until golden brown or until juices run clear. Serves 4.

Cranberry Chicken

6 boneless, skinless chicken breast halves	
1 (16 ounce) can whole cranberry sauce	**455 g**
1 large tart apple, peeled, chopped	
⅓ cup chopped walnuts	**45 g**
1 teaspoon curry powder	**5 ml**

- Preheat oven to 350° (175° C).

- Place chicken in sprayed 9 x 13-inch (23 x 33 cm) baking pan and bake uncovered for 20 minutes. Combine cranberry sauce, apple, walnuts and curry powder in bowl and spoon over chicken.

- Bake uncovered for additional 25 minutes or until chicken juices run clear. Serves 6.

Spicy Chicken and Rice

3 cups cooked sliced chicken	**420 g**
2 cups cooked brown rice	**390 g**
1 (10 ounce) can fiesta nacho cheese soup	**280 g**
1 (10 ounce) can diced tomatoes and green chilies	**280 g**

- Preheat oven to 350° (175° C).

- Combine chicken, rice, soup, and tomatoes and green chilies in bowl and mix well. Spoon mixture into sprayed 3-quart (3L) baking dish.

- Cover and bake for 45 minutes. Serves 6.

Ranch Chicken

½ cup grated parmesan cheese	**50 g**
1½ cups corn flakes	**40 g**
1 (1 ounce) packet ranch-style salad dressing mix	**30 g**
2 pounds chicken drumsticks	**910 g**
½ cup (1 stick) butter, melted	**115 g**

- Preheat oven to 350° (175° C).

- Combine cheese, corn flakes and dressing mix in bowl.

- Dip washed, dried chicken in melted butter and dredge in corn flake mixture.

- Bake uncovered for 50 minutes or until golden brown.
  Serves 4 to 6.

Sunday Chicken

5 - 6 boneless, skinless chicken breast halves	
½ cup sour cream	**120 g**
¼ cup soy sauce	**60 ml**
1 (10 ounce) can French onion soup	**280 g**

- Preheat oven to 350° (175° C).

- Place chicken in sprayed 9 x 13-inch (23 x 33 cm) baking dish.

- Combine sour cream, soy sauce and soup in saucepan and heat just enough to mix well. Pour over chicken breasts.

- Cover and bake for 55 minutes. Serves 5 to 6.

Chicken and Wild Rice Special

1 (6 ounce) package long grain-wild rice mix   170 g
4 - 5 boneless, skinless chicken breast halves
Canola oil
2 (10 ounce) cans French onion soup   2 (280 g)
1 red bell pepper, seeded, julienned
1 green bell pepper, seeded, julienned

- Cook rice according to package directions and keep warm.

- Brown chicken breasts on both sides with a little oil in large skillet over medium-high heat.

- Add soup, ¾ cup (175 ml) water and bell peppers. Reduce heat to medium-low, cover and cook for 15 minutes.

- To serve, place rice on serving platter and place chicken breasts on top. Serve sauce in gravy boat to pour over chicken and rice. Serves 4 to 5.

TIP: For a thicker sauce, spoon 2 or 3 tablespoons (30 or 45 ml) sauce in small bowl and stir in 2 tablespoons (15 g) flour. Mix well and stir into sauce. Heat and stir constantly until sauce thickens.

Lemonade Chicken

6 boneless, skinless chicken breast halves
1 (6 ounce) can frozen lemonade concentrate, thawed   **180 ml**
⅓ cup soy sauce   **75 ml**
1 teaspoon garlic powder   **5 ml**

- Preheat oven to 350° (175° C).

- Place chicken in sprayed 9 x 13-inch (23 x 33 cm) baking dish. Combine lemonade, soy sauce and garlic powder in bowl and pour over chicken.

- Cover and bake for 45 minutes. Pour juices over chicken and bake uncovered for additional 10 minutes. Serves 6.

Grilled Chicken Cordon Bleu

6 boneless, skinless chicken breast halves
6 slices Swiss cheese
6 thin slices deli ham
3 tablespoons canola oil   **45 ml**
1 cup seasoned breadcrumbs   **120 g**

- Flatten chicken to ¼-inch (6 mm) thickness and place 1 slice each of cheese and ham on each piece of chicken to within ¼ inch (6 mm) of edges.

- Fold in half and secure with toothpicks. Brush chicken with oil and roll in breadcrumbs. Grill, covered, over medium heat for 15 to 18 minutes or until juices run clear. Serves 6.

Dad's Best Smoked Chicken

3 whole chickens, cut in half	
½ cup (1 stick) butter	**230 g**
2 teaspoons Worcestershire sauce	**10 ml**
2 dashes hot sauce	
2 tablespoons lemon juice	**30 ml**
½ teaspoon garlic salt	**2 ml**
1 (12 ounce) can lemon-lime carbonated drink	**355 ml**

- Sprinkle chickens with pepper and leave at room temperature for 1 hour.

- Melt butter in small saucepan and add Worcestershire sauce, hot sauce, lemon juice, garlic salt and lemon-lime carbonated drink.

- Cook chickens over low charcoal fire with hickory or mesquite chips around sides of fire. Turn often and baste with sauce mixture several times.

- When chicken is done (about 60 minutes), baste once more to keep chicken moist. Serves 12.

Italian Chicken and Rice

3 boneless, chicken breasts halves, cut into strips	
1 (14 ounce) can chicken broth seasoned with	
Italian herbs	**395 g**
¾ cup rice	**140 g**
¼ cup grated parmesan cheese	**25 g**

- Cook chicken in non-stick skillet until brown, stirring often, and set aside.

- Add broth and rice to skillet and heat to boil. Cover and simmer over low heat for 25 minutes. (Add water if needed.) Stir in cheese and return chicken to pan. Cover and cook for 5 minutes or until done. Serves 6.

Chile Pepper Chicken

5 boneless, skinless chicken breast halves	
1 (1 ounce) package hot-and-spicy coating mixture	**30 g**
1 (4 ounce) can diced green chilies	**115 g**
Chunky salsa	

- Preheat oven to 375° (190 C).

- Dredge chicken in coating mixture and place in sprayed 9 x 13-inch (23 x 33 cm) baking dish.

- Bake for 25 minutes. Remove from oven, spread green chilies over chicken breasts and return to oven for 5 minutes. Serve with salsa over each chicken breast. Serves 5.

Lemony Chicken and Noodles

1 (8 ounce) package wide egg noodles	230 g
1 (10 ounce) package frozen sugar snap peas, thawed	280 g
1 (14 ounce) can chicken broth	395 g
1 teaspoon grated lemon peel	5 ml
2 cups cubed, skinless rotisserie chicken meat	280 g
½ cup whipping cream	125 ml

- Cook noodles according to package directions, but add snap peas to noodles 1 minute before noodles are done. Drain and return to saucepan.

- Add chicken broth, lemon peel, chicken, and ½ teaspoon (2 ml) each of salt and pepper. Heat, stirring constantly, until thoroughly hot.

- Over low heat, gently stir in cream. Serve hot. Serves 4 to 6.

Sweet-and-Sour Chicken

6 - 8 boneless, skinless chicken breast halves
Canola oil
1 (1 ounce) packet onion soup mix   **30 g**
1 (6 ounce) can frozen orange juice concentrate, thawed   175 ml

- Preheat oven to 350° (175° C).

- Brown chicken in a little oil or butter and place in sprayed
  9 x 13-inch (23 x 33 cm) baking dish.

- Combine soup mix, orange juice and ⅔ cup (150 ml) water in
  bowl, mix well and pour over chicken.

- Bake uncovered for 45 to 50 minutes. Serves 6 to 8.

Crispy Nutty Chicken

⅓ cup dry-roasted peanuts, minced   **50 g**
1 cup corn flake crumbs   **30 g**
½ cup ranch-style buttermilk salad dressing   **125 ml**
6 boneless, skinless chicken breast halves

- Preheat oven to 350° (175° C).

- Combine peanuts and crumbs on wax paper.

- Pour dressing into pie pan, dip each piece of chicken in dressing
  and roll chicken in crumb mixture to coat.

- Arrange chicken in shallow 9 x 13-inch (23 x 33 cm) baking dish.
  Bake uncovered for 50 minutes or until light brown. Serves 6.

Stir-Fry Chicken Spaghetti

1 (1 pound) boneless, skinless chicken breast halves	455 g
Canola oil	
1½ cups sliced mushrooms	110 g
1½ cups bell pepper strips	140 g
1 cup sweet-and-sour stir-fry sauce	250 ml
1 (16 ounce) package spaghetti, cooked	455 g
¼ cup (½ stick) butter	60 g

- Season chicken with a little salt and pepper and cut into thin slices. Brown chicken slices in large skillet with a little oil and cook for 5 minutes on medium-low heat. Transfer to plate and set aside.

- In same skillet with a little more oil, stir-fry mushrooms and bell pepper strips for 5 minutes. Add chicken strips and sweet-and-sour sauce and stir until ingredients are hot.

- While spaghetti is still hot, drain well, add butter and stir until butter melts. Place in large bowl and toss with chicken mixture. Serve hot. Serves 5.

To quickly slice mushrooms, small tomatoes, radishes and similar firm fruits and vegetables, use an egg slicer.

Hawaiian Chicken

2 small whole chickens, quartered
Flour
Canola oil
1 (20 ounce) can sliced pineapple with juice   **570 g**
2 bell peppers, cut in strips
Rice, cooked

- Preheat oven to 350° (175° C).

- Wash and pat chicken dry with paper towels. Mix flour and a little salt and pepper in bowl. Coat chicken with flour mixture, brown in oil and place in shallow pan.

- Drain pineapple into 2-cup (500 ml) measure, add enough water (or orange juice, if you have it) to make 1½ cups (375 ml) liquid and set aside.

Sauce for Hawaiian Chicken:

1 cup sugar	**200 g**
3 tablespoons cornstarch	**25 g**
¾ cup vinegar	**175 ml**
1 tablespoon lemon juice	**15 ml**
1 tablespoon soy sauce	**15 ml**
2 teaspoons chicken bouillon granules	**10 ml**

- Combine reserved 1½ cups (375 ml) juice with sauce ingredients in medium saucepan. Bring to boil and stir constantly until thick and clear, then pour over chicken. Bake covered 40 minutes.

- Place pineapple slices and bell peppers on top of chicken and bake uncovered for additional 10 minutes. Serve over rice. Serves 6.

Apricot Chicken

1 cup apricot preserves	320 g
1 (8 ounce) bottle Catalina salad dressing	250 ml
1 (1 ounce) packet onion soup mix	30 g
6 - 8 boneless, skinless chicken breast halves	
Rice, cooked	

- Preheat oven to 325° (165° C).

- Combine apricot preserves, salad dressing and soup mix in bowl. Place chicken breasts in large, sprayed baking dish and pour apricot mixture over chicken. (For a change of pace, use Russian dressing instead of Catalina).

- Bake uncovered for 1 hour 20 minutes. Serve over rice. Serves 6 to 8.

Catalina Chicken

6 - 8 boneless, skinless chicken breast halves	
1 (8 ounce) bottle Catalina salad dressing	250 ml
1½ cups crushed cracker crumbs	90 g

- Marinate chicken breasts in dressing for 3 to 4 hours and discard marinade.

- When ready to bake, preheat oven to 350° (175° C).

- Combine 1 teaspoon (5 ml) pepper and cracker crumbs in bowl. Dip each chicken breasts in crumb mixture and place in large, sprayed baking dish. Bake uncovered for 1 hour. Serves 6 to 8.

One-Dish Chicken Bake

1 (1 ounce) packet vegetable soup mix	**30 g**
1 (6 ounce) package chicken stuffing mix	**170 g**
4 boneless, skinless chicken breast halves	
1 (10 ounce) can cream of mushroom soup	**280 g**
⅓ cup sour cream	**80 ml**

- Preheat oven to 375° (190° C).

- Combine soup mix, stuffing mix and 1⅔ cups (400 ml) water and set aside.

- Place chicken in sprayed 9 x 13-inch (23 x 33 cm) baking dish.

- Mix soup and sour cream in saucepan over low heat just enough to pour over chicken. Spoon stuffing mixture evenly over top.

- Bake uncovered for 40 minutes. Serves 4.

It is best to marinate whole chickens overnight. Boneless breast halves take up to 3 hours in marinade to reach full flavor.

Favorite Chicken Breasts

6 - 8 boneless, skinless chicken breast halves	
1 (10 ounce) can golden mushroom soup	**280 g**
1 cup white wine	**250 ml**
1 (8 ounce) carton sour cream	**230 g**
Rice, cooked	

- Preheat oven to 350° (175° C).

- Place chicken breasts in large, shallow baking pan, sprinkle with a little salt and pepper, and bake uncovered for 30 minutes.

- Combine soup, wine and sour cream in saucepan and heat just enough to mix well.

- Remove chicken from oven and cover with soup mixture.

- Reduce oven to 300° (150°C) and bake for additional 30 minutes. Baste twice.

- Serve over rice. Serves 6 to 8.

Chicken Bake

8 boneless, skinless chicken breast halves
8 slices Swiss cheese
1 (10 ounce) can cream of chicken soup   **280 g**
1 (8 ounce) box chicken stuffing mix   **230 g**

- Preheat oven to 325° (165° C).

- Flatten chicken breasts with rolling pin and place in sprayed 9 x 13-inch (23 x 33 cm) baking dish.

- Place cheese slices over chicken.

- Combine chicken soup and ½ cup (125 ml) water in bowl and pour over chicken.

- Prepare stuffing mix according to package directions and sprinkle over chicken.

- Bake uncovered for 1 hour. Serves 8.

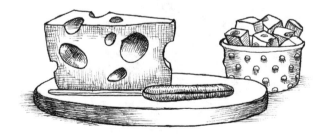

Mozzarella Cutlets

4 boneless, skinless chicken breast halves
1 cup Italian-seasoned breadcrumbs **120 g**
1 cup spaghetti sauce **250 g**
4 slices mozzarella cheese

- Preheat oven to 350° (175° C).

- Pound each chicken breast to flatten slightly.

- Coat chicken well in breadcrumbs and arrange in sprayed
  9 x 13-inch (23 x 33 cm) baking dish.

- Spread one-fourth spaghetti sauce over each portion.

- Place 1 slice cheese over each and garnish with remaining
  breadcrumbs.

- Bake uncovered for 45 minutes. Serves 4.

Jiffy Chicken

8 boneless, skinless chicken breast halves
¾ cup mayonnaise   **170 g**
2 cups crushed corn flakes   **55 g**
½ cup grated parmesan cheese   **50 g**

- Preheat oven to 325° (165° C).

- Sprinkle chicken breasts with a little salt and pepper.

- Dip chicken in mayonnaise and spread over chicken with brush.

- Combine corn flake crumbs and cheese in bowl and dip chicken in corn flake mixture until it coats completely.

- Place chicken in sprayed 9 x 13-inch (23 x 33 cm) glass baking dish and bake uncovered for 1 hour. Serves 8.

Honey-Baked Chicken

2 whole chickens, quartered	
½ cup (1 stick) butter, melted	**115 g**
⅔ cup honey	**230 g**
¼ cup dijon-style mustard	**60 g**
1 teaspoon curry powder	**5 ml**

- Preheat oven to 350° (175° C).

- Place chicken pieces skin side up in large, shallow baking dish and sprinkle with a little salt.

- Combine butter, honey, mustard and curry powder in bowl and pour over chicken.

- Bake uncovered for 1 hour 5 minutes and baste every 20 minutes. Serves 6.

Party Chicken Breasts

6 - 8 boneless, skinless chicken breast halves	
6 - 8 strips bacon	
1 (2.5 ounce) jar dried beef	**70 g**
1 (10 ounce) can cream of chicken soup	**280 g**
1 (8 ounce) carton sour cream	**230 g**

- Preheat oven to 325° (165° C).

- Wrap each chicken breast with 1 strip bacon and secure with toothpicks.

- Place dried beef in sprayed, large, shallow baking pan and place chicken on top.

- Heat soup and sour cream in saucepan just enough to pour over chicken.

- Cover chicken with soup mixture and bake uncovered for 1 hour. Serves 6 to 8.

Bacon-Wrapped Chicken

6 boneless, skinless chicken breast halves
1 (8 ounce) carton whipped cream cheese with onion
  and chives 230 g
Butter
6 bacon strips

- Preheat oven to 375° (190° C).

- Flatten chicken to ½ inch (1.2 cm) thickness and spread one-sixth cream cheese over each piece.

- Dot with butter and sprinkle with a little salt. Roll and wrap each with 1 bacon strip.

- Place seam-side down in sprayed 9 x 13-inch (23 x 33 cm) baking dish and bake uncovered for 40 to 45 minutes or until juices run clear.

- To brown, broil 6 inches (15 cm) from heat for about 3 minutes or until bacon is crisp. Serves 6.

Always cook with thicker slices of bacon. Thin strips will
fall apart when stretched around a chicken breast half.
Don't forget to tell your guests that you used toothpicks to
secure the meat so they can remove them before they eat.

Broccoli-Cheese Chicken

4 boneless, skinless chicken breast halves
1 tablespoon butter   **15 ml**
1 (10 ounce) can broccoli-cheese soup   **280 g**
1 (10 ounce) package frozen broccoli spears   **280 g**
⅓ cup milk   **75 ml**
Rice, cooked

- Cook chicken in butter in skillet for 15 minutes or until brown on both sides, remove and set aside.

- In same skillet, combine soup, broccoli, milk and a little pepper and heat to boiling, return chicken to skillet and reduce heat to low.

- Cover and cook for additional 25 minutes or until chicken is no longer pink and broccoli is tender. Serve over rice. Serves 4.

Asparagus-Cheese Chicken

1 tablespoon butter	15 ml
4 boneless, skinless chicken breast halves	
1 (10 ounce) can broccoli-cheese soup	280 g
1 (10 ounce) package frozen asparagus cuts	280 g
⅓ cup milk	75 ml

- Heat butter in skillet and cook chicken for 10 to 15 minutes or until brown on both sides.

- Remove chicken and set aside.

- In same skillet, combine soup, asparagus and milk and heat to a boil.

- Return chicken to skillet, reduce heat to low, cover and cook for additional 25 minutes until chicken is no longer pink and asparagus is tender. Serves 4.

Cheesy Chicken and Potatoes

Canola oil
1 (20 ounce) package frozen hash browns with
    peppers and onions, thawed   570 g
1 tablespoon minced garlic   15 ml
2 - 2½ cups bite-size chunks rotisserie chicken   280 - 350 g
1 bunch green onions, sliced
1 cup shredded cheddar cheese   115 g

- Add a little oil to large skillet over medium-high heat; cook potatoes for 7 minutes and turn frequently.

- Add garlic, chicken, green onions and ⅓ cup (75 ml) water and cook for 5 to 6 minutes. Remove from heat and stir in cheese. Serve immediately right from skillet. Serves 4 to 6.

After-Thanksgiving Turkey Chili

3 pounds ground turkey   1.4 kg
½ teaspoon garlic powder   2 ml
3 tablespoons chili powder   25 g
1 (8 ounce) can tomato sauce   230 g
Shredded cheese

- Combine turkey, garlic powder and 1 cup (250 ml) water to large saucepan. Cook over medium heat until mixture begins to fry.

- Add chili powder and tomato sauce and simmer until meat is tender. Garnish with cheese. Serves 6 to 8.

PORK
MAIN DISHES

Pork Main Dishes Contents

Look for baking dishes with lids. Any leftovers can be refrigerated right in the pan they were baked in and cleanup is a snap!

Orange Pork Chops

6 (½ inch) thick boneless pork chops	6 (1.2 cm)
2 tablespoons canola oil	30 ml
1⅓ cups instant rice	130 g
1 cup orange juice	250 ml
¼ teaspoon ground ginger	1 ml
1 (10 ounce) can condensed chicken and rice soup	280 g
½ cup chopped walnuts	65 g

- Preheat oven to 350° (175° C).

- Sprinkle a little salt and pepper over pork chops and brown in skillet with oil.

- Sprinkle rice into sprayed 7 x 11-inch (18 x 28 cm) baking dish. Add orange juice and arrange pork chops over rice.

- Add ginger to soup and stir right in can. Pour soup over pork chops. Sprinkle walnuts over pork chops.

- Cover and bake for 25 minutes.

- Uncover and bake for additional 10 minutes or until rice is tender. Serves 6.

Pineapple Pork Chops

6 - 8 thick, boneless pork chops
Canola oil
1 (6 ounce) can frozen pineapple juice concentrate,
    thawed   **175 ml**
3 tablespoons brown sugar   **40 g**
⅓ cup wine or tarragon vinegar   **75 ml**
⅓ cup honey   **115 g**
Rice, cooked

- Preheat oven to 325° (165° C). Place pork chops in a little oil in skillet and brown. Remove to shallow baking dish.

- Combine remaining ingredients in bowl and pour over chops. Cover and cook for about 50 minutes. Serve over rice. Serves 6 to 8.

Pork Chops in Cream Gravy

4 (¼ inch) thick pork chops   **4 (6 mm)**
Flour
Canola oil
2¼ cups milk   **560 ml**
Rice, cooked

- Trim all fat off pork chops. Dip chops in flour mixed with a little salt and pepper. Brown pork chops on both sides in a little oil in skillet. Remove chops from skillet.

- Add about 2 tablespoons (15 g) flour to skillet, brown lightly and stir in a little salt and pepper. Slowly stir in milk to make gravy.

- Return chops to skillet with gravy. Cover and simmer on low for about 40 minutes. Serve over rice. Serves 4.

Spicy Pork Chops

4 - 6 pork chops
Canola oil
1 large onion
1 bell pepper
1 (10 ounce) can diced tomatoes and green chilies   280 g

- Preheat oven to 350° (175° C).

- Brown pork chops in skillet with a little oil. Place chops in sprayed baking dish.

- Cut onion and bell pepper into large chunks and place on chops. Pour tomato and green chilies over chops and sprinkle with 1 teaspoon (5 ml) salt.

- Cover and bake for 45 minutes. Serves 4 to 6.

Pork Casserole

4 - 5 potatoes, peeled, sliced
6 pork chops
1 (10 ounce) can fiesta nacho cheese soup   280 g
½ soup can milk

- Preheat oven to 350° (175° C). Place potatoes in sprayed baking dish and place pork chops on top.

- Combine soup and milk in saucepan and heat just enough to pour over chops. Cover and bake for 45 minutes. Uncover and bake for additional 15 minutes. Serves 6.

Pork Chops and Apples

Simple and delicious!

6 thick-cut pork chops
Flour
Canola oil
3 baking apples

- Preheat oven to 325° (165° C).

- Dip pork chops in flour and coat well.

- Brown pork chops in oil in skillet and place in sprayed
  9 x 13-inch (23 x 33 cm) baking dish. Add ⅓ cup (75 ml)
  water to casserole. Cover and bake for 50 minutes.

- Peel, halve and seed apples and place half apple over each pork
  chop. Return to oven for 10 minutes. (Don't overcook apples.)
  Serves 6.

Tangy Pork Chops

4 - 6 pork chops	
¼ cup Worcestershire sauce	**60 ml**
¼ cup ketchup	**70 g**
½ cup honey	**170 g**

- Preheat oven to 325° (165° C). Brown pork chops in skillet and
  remove to shallow baking dish.

- Combine Worcestershire, ketchup and honey in bowl and pour
  over pork chops. Cover and bake for 45 minutes. Serves 4 to 6.

Oven Pork Chops

6 - 8 medium-thick pork chops
Canola oil
1 (10 ounce) can cream of chicken soup   **280 g**
3 tablespoons ketchup   **50 g**
1 tablespoon Worcestershire sauce   **15 ml**
1 medium onion, chopped

- Preheat oven to 350° (175° C).

- Brown pork chops in a little oil in skillet, season with a little salt and pepper and place drained pork chops in shallow baking dish.

- Combine soup, ketchup, Worcestershire and onion in saucepan, heat just enough to mix and pour over pork chops.

- Cover and bake for 35 minutes. Uncover and bake for additional 15 minutes. Serves 6 to 8.

Onion-Smothered Pork Chops

6 (½ inch) thick pork chops	6 (1.2 cm)
1 tablespoon canola oil	15 ml
2 tablespoons butter	30 g
1 onion, chopped	
1 (10 ounce) can cream of onion soup	280 g
Brown rice, cooked	

- Preheat oven to 325° (165° C).

- Brown pork chops in oil in skillet, simmer for about 10 minutes and place pork chops in sprayed shallow baking pan.

- In same skillet, add butter and saute chopped onion. (Pan juices are brown from pork chops so onions will be brown from juices already in skillet.)

- Add onion soup and ½ cup (125 ml) water and stir well. (Sauce will have a nice light brown color.)

- Pour onion mixture over pork chops. Cover and bake for 40 minutes and serve over brown rice. Serves 6.

Praline Ham

2 (½ inch) thick ham slices, cooked (about 2½ pounds)	**2 (1.2 cm)/1.1 kg**
½ cup maple syrup	**125 ml**
3 tablespoons brown sugar	**40 g**
1 tablespoon butter	**15 ml**
⅓ cup chopped pecans	**35 g**

- Preheat oven to 325° (165° C). Bake ham slices in shallow pan for 10 minutes.

- Bring syrup, brown sugar and butter to a boil in small saucepan and stir often. Stir in pecans and spoon syrup mixture over ham. Bake for additional 20 minutes. Serves 4.

Peachy Glazed Ham

1 (15 ounce) can sliced peaches in light syrup with juice	**425 g**
2 tablespoons dark brown sugar	**30 g**
2 teaspoons dijon-style mustard	**10 ml**
1 (1 pound) center-cut ham slice	**455 g**
⅓ cup sliced green onions	**30 g**

- Drain peaches, reserve ½ cup (125 ml) juice in large skillet and set peaches aside.

- Add brown sugar and mustard to skillet; bring to a boil over medium-high heat and cook for 2 minutes or until slightly reduced.

- Add ham and for cook 2 minutes on each side. Add peaches and green onions, cover and cook over low heat for 3 minutes or until peaches are thoroughly hot. Serves 4 to 6.

Baked Ham and Pineapple

1 (6 - 8 pound) fully cooked, bone-in ham	2.7 - 3.6 kg
Whole cloves	
½ cup packed brown sugar	110 g
1 (8 ounce) can sliced pineapple with juice	230 g
5 maraschino cherries	

- Preheat oven to 325° (165° C).

- Place ham in roasting pan, score surface with shallow diagonal cuts making diamond shapes and insert cloves into diamonds.

- Cover and bake for 1 hour 30 minutes.

- Combine brown sugar and juice from pineapple in bowl and pour over ham.

- Arrange pineapple slices and cherries on ham. Bake uncovered for additional 40 minutes. Serves 10 to 12.

Apricot-Baked Ham

1 (12 - 20 pound) whole ham, fully cooked	5.4 - 9 kg
Whole cloves	
2 tablespoons dry mustard	30 ml
1¼ cups apricot jam	400 g
1¼ cups packed light brown sugar	275 g

- Preheat oven to 450° (230° C).

- Place ham on rack in large roasting pan and insert cloves into ham every inch or so.

- Combine dry mustard and jam in bowl and spread over entire surface of ham.

- Pat brown sugar over jam mixture. Reduce heat to 325° (165° C) and bake uncovered for 15 minutes per pound. Serves 10 to 12.

Pineapple Sauce for Ham

Pre-sliced, cooked honey-baked ham slices	
1 (15 ounce) can pineapple chunks with juice	425 g
1 cup apricot preserves	320 g
1¼ cups packed brown sugar	275 g
¼ teaspoon cinnamon	1 ml

- Place ham slices in shallow baking pan. Combine pineapple, preserves, brown sugar and cinnamon in saucepan and heat.

- Pour sauce over ham slices and heat.

Walnut-Ham Linguine

2 teaspoons minced garlic	**10 ml**
½ cup coarsely chopped walnuts	**65 g**
1 red bell pepper, thinly slice	
¼ cup olive oil	**60 ml**
½ pound cooked ham, cut in strips	**230 g**
1 (16 ounce) jar creamy alfredo sauce	**455 g**
¼ cup grated parmesan cheese	**25 g**
1 (12 ounce) package linguine, cooked al dente	**340 g**
1 cup seasoned breadcrumbs	**120 g**

- Preheat oven to 350° (175° C).

- Saute garlic, walnuts and bell pepper in oil in large skillet for 1 to 2 minutes.

- Combine garlic-bell pepper mixture, ham, alfredo sauce, parmesan cheese and linguine in large bowl and mix well.

- Spoon into sprayed 3-quart (3 L) baking dish. Sprinkle breadcrumbs over top.

- Bake uncovered for 35 minutes or until breadcrumbs are light brown. Serves 6 to 8.

Ham and Potatoes Olé!

1 (24 ounce) package frozen hash browns with onion and peppers, thawed	680 g
3 cups cubed, cooked ham	420 g
1 (10 ounce) can cream of chicken soup	280 g
1 (10 ounce) can fiesta nacho cheese soup	280 g
1 cup hot salsa	265 g
1 (8 ounce) package shredded cheddar-Jack cheese	230 g

- Preheat oven to 350° (175° C). Combine potatoes, ham, soups and salsa in large bowl and mix well. Spoon into sprayed 9 x 13-inch (23 x 33 cm) baking dish.

- Cover and bake for 40 minutes. Sprinkle cheese over casserole and bake uncovered for additional 5 minutes. Serves 6 to 8.

Sausage Casserole

1 pound pork sausage	455 g
2 (15 ounce) cans pork and beans	2 (425 g)
1 (15 ounce) can Mexican stewed tomatoes	425 g
1 (8 ounce) package cornbread muffin mix	230 g

- Preheat oven to 400° (205° C). Brown sausage in skillet and drain fat. Add beans and tomatoes, blend and bring to a boil. Pour mixture into sprayed 3-quart (3 L) baking dish.

- Prepare muffin mix according to package directions and drop teaspoonfuls of mixture over meat-bean mixture. Bake for 30 minutes or until top browns. Serves 6.

Sandwich Souffle

A fun lunch!

Butter, softened
8 slices white bread, crusts removed
4 slices ham
4 slices American cheese
2 cups milk   **500 ml**
2 eggs, beaten

- Butter bread on both sides, make 4 sandwiches with ham and cheese. Place sandwiches in sprayed 8-inch (20 cm) square baking pan.

- Beat milk, eggs, and a little salt and pepper in bowl. Pour over sandwiches and soak for 1 to 2 hours in refrigerator.

- When ready to bake, preheat oven to 375° (190° C).

- Bake for 45 to 50 minutes. Serves 4.

Grilled Pork Loin

1 (4 pound) boneless pork loin roast	1.8 kg
1 (8 ounce) bottle Italian salad dressing	250 ml
1 cup dry white wine	250 ml
3 cloves garlic, minced	
10 black peppercorns	

- Pierce roast at 1-inch (2.5 cm) intervals with fork and set aside.

- Combine salad dressing, wine, garlic and peppercorns in bowl. Refrigerate ½ cup (125 ml) mixture for basting during grilling.

- Place roast in large, resealable plastic bag with remaining mixture, refrigerate for 8 hours and turn occasionally.

- Remove roast from marinade and discard marinade.

- Place roast on rack on grill.

- Cook, covered with grill lid, for 35 minutes or until meat thermometer inserted into thickest portion reaches 160° (70° C). Turn occasionally and baste with ½ cup (125 ml) reserved marinade mixture. Serves 6 to 8.

Lemonade Spareribs

4 pounds pork spareribs	**1.8 kg**
1 (6 ounce) can frozen lemonade concentrate, thawed	**175 ml**
½ teaspoon garlic salt	**2 ml**
⅓ cup soy sauce	**75 ml**

- Preheat oven to 350° (175° C).

- Place ribs, meaty-side down, in shallow roasting pan. Cover and bake for 40 minutes.

- Drain fat and bake for additional 30 minutes. Drain fat again.

- Combine lemonade concentrate, garlic salt and soy sauce in bowl and brush on ribs.

- Reduce oven to 325° (165° C), cover and bake for additional 1 hour or until ribs are tender. Brush occasionally with sauce. Serves 4 to 6.

Tequila Baby-Back Ribs

4 pounds baby-back pork ribs	1.8 kg
1 (12 ounce) bottle tequila-lime marinade, divided	355 ml

- Cut ribs in lengths to fit in large, resealable plastic bag.

- Place ribs, add ¾ cup (175 ml) marinade and a little pepper in bag and shake to coat. Refrigerate overnight.

- When ready to bake, preheat oven to 375° (190° C).

- Place ribs in sprayed shallow baking dish and discard marinade.

- Cover and bake for 30 minutes. Spread remaining marinade over ribs.

- Reduce oven to 300° (150° C). Cover and bake for 1 hour. Uncover to let ribs brown and bake for additional 30 minutes. Serves 4 to 6.

Hawaiian Aloha Pork

This is great served over rice.

1 (2 pound) lean pork tenderloin, cut into 1-inch cubes	910 g/2.5 cm
1 (15 ounce) can pineapple chunks with juice	425 g
1 (12 ounce) bottle chili sauce	340 g
1 teaspoon ground ginger	5 ml

- Season pork with a little salt and pepper in skillet. Add pineapple with juice, chili sauce and ginger. Cover and simmer for 1 hour 30 minutes. Serves 4 to 6.

One-Dish Pork and Peas

So many of our casseroles are chicken, but pork is so good and always tender. This blend of ingredients makes a delicious dish.

2 pounds pork tenderloin	**910 g**
2 tablespoons canola oil, divided	**30 ml**
1½ cups celery, sliced	**150 g**
1 large onion, chopped	
2 red bell peppers, seeded, chopped	
1 (12 ounce) package small egg noodles, cooked, drained	**340 g**
1 (10 ounce) can cream of chicken soup	**280 g**
1 (10 ounce) can chicken broth	**280 g**
1 (8 ounce) carton whipping cream	**250 ml**
1 (10 ounce) package frozen green peas, thawed	**280 g**
1½ cups seasoned breadcrumbs	**180 g**
¾ cup chopped walnuts	**100 g**

- Preheat oven to 350° (175° C).

- Cut pork tenderloin into ½-inch (1.2 cm) cubes. Brown pork in 1 tablespoon (15 ml) oil in large skillet. Reduce heat and cook for 25 minutes. Remove pork to separate dish. In remaining oil, saute celery, onion and bell pepper.

- Add pork, noodles, soup, broth, whipping cream, peas, 1½ teaspoons (7 ml) salt and 1 teaspoon (5 ml) pepper; mix well. Spoon into sprayed 10 x 15-inch (25 x 38 cm) baking dish. Sprinkle with breadcrumbs and walnuts.

- Bake uncovered for 35 to 45 minutes or until bubbly around edges and breadcrumbs are light brown. Serves 20.

Creamy Fettuccini

1 (8 ounce) package fettuccini	230 g
1 pound Italian sausage	455 g
1 (10 ounce) can cream of mushroom soup	280 g
1 (16 ounce) carton sour cream	455 g

- Preheat oven to 325° (165° C).

- Cook fettuccini according to package directions and drain.

- Cut sausage into ½-inch (1.2 cm) pieces, brown in skillet over medium heat, cook for 8 minutes and drain.

- Combine all ingredients in bowl and pour into sprayed 2-quart (2 L) baking dish. Bake for 30 minutes. Serves 6.

Sweet-and-Sour Spareribs

3 - 4 pounds spareribs	1.4 - 1.8 kg
3 tablespoons soy sauce	45 ml
⅓ cup mustard	85 g
1 cup packed brown sugar	220 g
½ teaspoon garlic salt	2 ml

- Preheat oven to 325° (165° C).

- Place spareribs in roasting pan, bake for 45 minutes and drain.

- To make sauce, combine soy sauce, mustard, brown sugar and garlic salt in bowl and brush on ribs.

- Return to oven, reduce heat to 300° (150° C) and bake for 2 hours or until ribs are tender. Baste several times. Serve 4 to 6.

Tenderloin with Apricot Sauce

3 pounds pork tenderloins	1.4 kg
1 cup apricot preserves	320 g
⅓ cup lemon juice	75 ml
⅓ cup ketchup	90 g
1 tablespoon soy sauce	15 ml
Rice, cooked	

- Preheat oven to 325° (165° C).

- Place tenderloins in roasting pan. Combine preserves, lemon juice, ketchup and soy sauce in bowl.

- Pour preserve mixture over pork. Cover and bake for 1 hour 20 minutes. Baste once. Serve over rice. Serves 6 to 8.

SEAFOOD MAIN DISHES

Seafood Main Dishes Contents

The best way to keep cleaned fish from getting freezer burn is to fill a plastic bag about half full of water. Add fish and add more water so fish is covered. Seal and record the date the fish is frozen.

Crispy Fish and Cheese Fillets

2 pounds fish fillets	910 g
½ cup creamy ranch-style salad dressing	125 ml
1½ cups crushed cheese crackers	90 g
2 tablespoons butter, melted	30 g

- Preheat oven to 425° (220° C).

- Cut fish into serving portions, dip into dressing and roll in cracker crumbs.

- Place in sprayed shallow pan and drizzle butter over fish. Bake uncovered for 15 minutes or until fish flakes easily. Serves 4 to 5.

Baked Fish

1 pound fish fillets	455 g
¼ cup butter, divided	60 g
1 teaspoon tarragon	5 ml
2 teaspoons capers	10 ml
2 tablespoons lemon juice	30 ml

- Preheat oven to 375° (190° C).

- Place fish fillets and 1 tablespoon (15 ml) butter in sprayed shallow pan and sprinkle with a little salt and pepper.

- Bake for about 5 to 6 minutes, turn and bake for additional 4 to 6 minutes or until fish flakes.

- For sauce, melt remaining butter with tarragon, capers and lemon juice in saucepan and serve over warm fish. Serves 3 to 4.

Chips and Fish

3 - 4 fish fillets, rinsed, dried
1 cup mayonnaise   **225 g**
2 tablespoons fresh lime juice   **30 ml**
1½ cups crushed corn chips   **130 g**
Lime wedges

- Preheat oven to 425° (220° C).

- Mix mayonnaise and lime juice in bowl and spread on both sides of fish fillets.

- Place crushed corn chips on wax paper, dredge both sides of fish in chips and shake off excess chips.

- Place fillets on foil-covered baking sheet and bake for 15 minutes or until fish flakes. Serve with lime wedges. Serves 3 to 4.

There is usually a thin end on most fish fillets. When cooking fillets, wrap the thin end over the fillet until it is about the same thickness as the thicker end.

Golden Catfish Fillets

3 eggs	
¾ cup flour	**90 g**
¾ cup cornmeal	**120 g**
1 teaspoon garlic powder	**5 ml**
6 - 8 (4 - 8 ounce) catfish fillets	**6 - 8 (115 - 230 g)**
Canola oil	

- Beat eggs in shallow bowl until foamy.

- In separate shallow bowl, combine flour, cornmeal, garlic powder and a little salt.

- Dip fillets in eggs and coat with cornmeal mixture.

- Heat ¼ inch (6 mm) oil in large skillet and fry fish over medium-high heat for about 4 minutes on each side or until fish flakes easily with fork. Serves 6 to 8.

The most important thing to remember about cooking fish is to not overcook it. The internal temperature should be about 145° and the flesh should be opaque and flake easily. Don't let fish dry out.

Flounder au Gratin

½ cup fine breadcrumbs	60 g
¼ cup grated parmesan cheese	25 g
1 pound flounder fillets	455 g
⅓ cup mayonnaise	75 g

- Preheat oven to 375° (190° C).

- Combine crumbs and cheese in shallow dish.

- Brush both sides of fish fillets with mayonnaise and coat with crumb mixture.

- Arrange fillets in single layer in shallow pan and bake for 20 to 25 minutes or until fish flakes easily. Serves 4.

Salmon Croquettes

1 (15 ounce) can pink salmon, drained, flaked	425 g
1 egg	
½ cup biscuit mix	60 g
¼ cup ketchup	70 g
Canola oil	

- Combine salmon (discard skin and bones) and egg in bowl.

- Add biscuit mix and ketchup and mix well. Shape into round patties (croquettes) about 2½ to 3 inches (6.4 to 8 cm) in diameter.

- Heat a little oil in skillet and place each croquette into skillet.

- Cook each side until brown. Serves 4.

Lemon-Dill Fillets

½ cup mayonnaise	110 g
2 tablespoons lemon juice	30 ml
½ teaspoon grated lemon peel	2 ml
1 teaspoon dill weed	5 ml
1 pound cod or flounder fillets	455 g

- Preheat grill or broiler.

- Combine mayonnaise, lemon juice, lemon peel and dill weed in bowl until they blend well.

- Place fish on sprayed grill or broiler rack and brush with half mayonnaise mixture.

- Grill or broil for 5 to 8 minutes, turn and brush with remaining mayonnaise mixture.

- Continue grilling or broiling for 5 to 8 minutes or until fish flakes easily with fork. Serves 4.

Flounder fillets will usually have intact skin In this case, look for skin with a glossy appearance. If the fish is whole, make sure the eye is clear, not foggy.

Lemon Baked Fish

1 pound sole or halibut fillets	**455 g**
3 tablespoons butter, divided	**45 g**
1 teaspoon dried tarragon	**5 ml**
2 tablespoons lemon juice	**30 ml**

- Preheat oven to 375° (190° C).

- Place fish fillets in sprayed shallow pan with 1 tablespoon (15 ml) butter and sprinkle with a little salt and pepper.

- Bake for 8 to 10 minutes, turn and bake for additional 6 minutes or until fish flakes.

- Melt 2 tablespoons (30 ml) butter with tarragon and lemon juice in saucepan and serve over warm fish fillets. Serves 3 to 4.

When buying a whole fish check to make sure the eyes are clear and the flesh is firm. When buying fillets or steaks, be sure flesh is uniform in color with no brown spots.

Baked Halibut

2 (1 inch) thick halibut steaks	**2 (2.5 cm)**
1 (8 ounce) carton sour cream	**230 g**
½ cup grated parmesan cheese	**50 g**
¾ teaspoon dill weed	**4 ml**
Paprika	

- Preheat oven to 325° (165° C).

- Place halibut in sprayed 9 x 13-inch (23 x 33 cm) baking dish.

- Combine sour cream, parmesan cheese and dill weed (and salt and pepper, if desired) in bowl and spoon over halibut.

- Cover and bake for 20 minutes.

- Sprinkle with paprika and bake uncovered for additional 10 minutes or until fish flakes easily with fork. Serves 2.

The halibut is a relative of the flounder, although a much, much larger one. Halibut are found in cold waters and can weigh as much as 600 pounds.

Orange Roughy with Peppers

1 pound orange roughy fillets	455 g
Canola oil	
1 onion, sliced	
2 red bell peppers, seeded, julienned	
1 teaspoon dried thyme, divided	5 ml

- Cut fish into 4 serving-size pieces.

- Heat a little oil in skillet, layer onion and bell peppers in oil and sprinkle with half thyme and ¼ teaspoon pepper.

- Place fish over peppers and sprinkle with remaining thyme.

- Turn burner on high just until fish begins to cook.

- Lower heat, cover and cook for 15 to 20 minutes or until fish flakes easily. Serves 3 to 4.

Chipper Fish

2 pounds sole or orange roughy	910 g
½ cup Caesar salad dressing	125 ml
1 cup crushed potato chips	55 g
½ cup shredded cheddar cheese	55 g

- Preheat oven to 375° (190° C).

- Dip fish in dressing and place in sprayed baking dish.

- Combine potato chips and cheese in bowl and sprinkle over fish.

- Bake for about 20 to 25 minutes. Serves 4 to 5.

Boiled Shrimp

3 pounds fresh shrimp	**1.4 kg**
2 teaspoons seafood seasoning	**10 ml**
½ cup vinegar	**125 ml**

- Remove heads from shrimp.

- Place all ingredients and 1 teaspoon (5 ml) salt in large saucepan, add enough water to cover shrimp and bring to a boil.

- Reduce heat and boil for 10 minutes.

- Remove from heat, drain and refrigerate. Serves 8.

Beer-Batter Shrimp

1 (12 ounce) can beer	**355 ml**
1 cup flour	**120 g**
2 teaspoons garlic powder	**10 ml**
1 pound shrimp, peeled, veined	**455 g**
Canola oil	

- Combine beer, flour and garlic powder in bowl and stir to creamy consistency to make batter.

- Dip shrimp into batter to cover and deep fry in hot oil. Serves 4.

Seafood Delight

1 (6 ounce) can shrimp, drained	170 g
1 (6 ounce) can crabmeat, drained, flaked	170 g
1 (10 ounce) can corn or potato chowder	280 g
2 - 3 cups seasoned breadcrumbs, divided	240 - 360 g

- Preheat oven to 350° (175° C).

- Mix shrimp, crabmeat, chowder and ⅓ cup (40 g) breadcrumbs in bowl.

- Place mixture in sprayed 1½-quart (1.5 L) baking dish and sprinkle with remaining breadcrumbs.

- Bake for 30 minutes or until casserole bubbles and breadcrumbs are light brown. Serves 4.

Creamed Shrimp over Rice

3 (10 ounce) cans cream of shrimp soup	3 (280 g)
1 (1 pint) carton sour cream	455 g
1½ teaspoons curry powder	7 ml
2 (5 ounce) cans veined shrimp	2 (145 g)
Rice, cooked	

- Combine all ingredients except rice in double boiler.

- Heat and stir constantly, but do not boil.

- Serve over rice. Serves 4.

Crabmeat Casserole

2 (6 ounce) cans crabmeat, drained, flaked	2 (170 g)
1 (3 ounce) can french-fried onions, divided	85 g
1 (10 ounce) can cream of chicken soup	280 g
¾ cup cracker crumbs	45 g

- Preheat oven to 350° (175° C).

- Combine crabmeat, half fried onions, soup and cracker crumbs in bowl and mix well.

- Place in sprayed baking dish and top with remaining onions. Cover and bake for 30 minutes. Serves 4 to 6.

Tuna and Chips

1 (6 ounce) can tuna, drained	170 g
1 (10 ounce) can cream of chicken soup	280 g
¾ cup milk	175 ml
1½ cups crushed potato chips, divided	85 g

- Preheat oven to 350° (175° C). Break chunks of tuna into bowl and stir in soup and milk. Add ¾ cup (40 g) crushed potato chips and mix well.

- Pour mixture into sprayed baking dish and sprinkle remaining chips over top.

- Bake uncovered for 30 minutes or until chips are light brown. Serves 4.

Crab Mornay

2 (6 ounce) cans crabmeat, drained	**2 (170 g)**
1 cup cream of mushroom soup	**250 ml**
½ cup shredded Swiss cheese	**55 g**
½ cup seasoned breadcrumbs	**60 g**

- Preheat oven to 350° (175° C).

- Combine crabmeat, soup and cheese in bowl and mix well.

- Pour into sprayed 1½-quart (1.5 L) baking dish and sprinkle with breadcrumbs.

- Bake uncovered for 30 minutes or until soup bubbles and breadcrumbs are brown. Serves 4.

Baked Oysters

1 cup oysters, drained, rinsed, divided	**160 g**
2 cups cracker crumbs, divided	**120 g**
¼ cup (½ stick) butter, melted, divided	**60 g**
½ cup milk, warmed	**125 ml**

- Preheat oven to 350° (175° C).

- Layer half oysters, half cracker crumbs and half butter in 7 x 11-inch (18 x 28 cm) baking dish. Repeat layers.

- Pour warmed milk over layers and add lots of salt and pepper.

- Bake for 35 minutes. Serves 4 to 6.

SWEETS

Sweets Contents

Pecan-Topped Toffee

1 cup (2 sticks) butter	**230 g**
1¼ cups packed brown sugar	**275 g**
6 (1.5 ounce) milk chocolate candy bars	**6 (45 g)**
⅔ cup finely chopped pecans	**75 g**

- Combine butter and brown sugar in saucepan and cook on medium-high heat.

- Stir constantly until mixture reaches 300° (150° C) on candy thermometer and pour immediately into sprayed 9-inch (23 cm) baking pan.

- Lay chocolate bars evenly over hot candy.

- When chocolate is soft, spread into smooth layer.

- Sprinkle pecans over chocolate and press lightly with back of spoon.

- Refrigerate for 1 hour.

- Invert candy onto wax paper and break into small, irregular pieces. Yields 1 quart (1 L).

Microwave Pralines

1½ cups packed brown sugar	330 g
⅔ cup half-and-half cream	150 ml
2 tablespoons butter, melted	30 g
1⅔ cups chopped pecans	185 g

• Combine brown sugar, half-and-half cream and dash of salt in deep glass dish and mix well. Blend in butter.

• Microwave on HIGH for 10 minutes, stir once and add pecans. Cool for 1 minute.

• Beat with spoon until creamy and thick, about 4 to 5 minutes. (The mixture will lose some of its gloss.)

• Drop tablespoonfuls of mixture onto wax paper. Yields 2 dozen.

Dream Candy

2 (8 ounce) cartons whipping cream	2 (250 ml)
3 cups sugar	600 g
1 cup light corn syrup	250 ml
1 cup chopped pecans	110 g

• Combine whipping cream, sugar and corn syrup in saucepan and cook to soft-ball stage (234°/112° C on candy thermometer).

• Stir and beat until candy is cool. Add pecans and pour into sprayed 9-inch (23 cm) pan. Serves 12 to 15.

Caramel Crunch

½ cup firmly packed brown sugar	110 g
½ cup light corn syrup	125 ml
¼ cup (½ stick) butter	60 g
6 cups bite-size crispy corn cereal squares	185 g
2 cups peanuts	290 g

- Preheat oven to 250° (120° C).

- Heat brown sugar, syrup and butter in large saucepan. Stir constantly until sugar and butter melt.

- Add cereal and peanuts and stir until all ingredients are well coated.

- Spread mixture on lightly sprayed baking sheet and bake for 30 minutes. Stir occasionally while baking.

- Cool and store in airtight container. Yields 2 quarts (2 L).

Peanut Brittle

2 cups sugar	400 g
½ cup light corn syrup	125 ml
2 cups dry-roasted peanuts	290 g
1 tablespoon butter	15 ml
1 teaspoon baking soda	5 ml

- Combine sugar and corn syrup in saucepan. Stir constantly over low heat until sugar dissolves. Cover and cook over medium heat for additional 2 minutes.

- Add peanuts and cook, stirring occasionally, to hard-crack stage 300° (150° C).

- Stir in butter and baking soda, pour into sprayed jellyroll pan and spread thinly. Cool and break into pieces. Yields 3 dozen pieces

White Chocolate Fudge

This is a little different slant to fudge; really creamy and really good!

1 (8 ounce) package cream cheese, softened	**230 g**
4 cups powdered sugar	**480 g**
1½ teaspoons vanilla	**7 ml**
1 (12 ounce) package almond bark, melted	**340 g**
¾ cup chopped pecans	**85 g**

- Beat cream cheese in bowl on medium speed until smooth, gradually add powdered sugar and vanilla and beat well.

- Stir in melted almond bark and pecans and spread into sprayed 8-inch (20 cm) square pan.

- Refrigerate until firm and cut into small squares. Yields 9 squares.

Diamond Fudge

1 (6 ounce) package semi-sweet chocolate chips	170 g
1 cup peanut butter	290 g
½ cup (1 stick) butter	115 g
1 cup powdered sugar	120 g

- Combine chocolate chips, peanut butter and butter in saucepan over low heat. Stir constantly, just until mixture melts and is smooth.

- Remove from heat, add powdered sugar and stir until smooth. Spoon into sprayed 8-inch (20 cm) square pan and refrigerate until firm.

- Let stand for 10 minutes at room temperature before cutting into squares. Store in refrigerator. Yields 9 squares.

Microwave Fudge

3 cups semi-sweet chocolate chips	510 g
1 (14 ounce) can sweetened condensed milk	395 g
¼ cup (½ stick) butter, sliced	60 g
1 cup chopped walnuts	130 g

- Combine chocolate chips, sweetened condensed milk and butter in 2-quart (2 L) glass bowl.

- Microwave on MEDIUM for 4 to 5 minutes and stir at 1½-minute intervals. Stir in walnuts and pour into sprayed 8-inch (20 cm) square dish. Refrigerate 2 hours and cut into squares. Yields 9 squares.

Pecan Squares

1 (24 ounce) package white almond bark	680 g
1 cup cinnamon chips	150 g
1 cup chopped pecans	110 g
8 cups frosted rice crispy cereal	210 g

- Melt almond bark and cinnamon chips in very large saucepan on low heat and stir constantly until they melt.

- Remove from heat and add pecans and cereal. Mix well and stir into 9 x 13-inch (23 x 33 cm) pan. Pat down with back of spoon, refrigerate just until set and cut into squares. Yields 12 squares.

Nutty Blonde Brownies

1 (16 ounce) box light brown sugar	455 g
4 eggs	
2 cups biscuit mix	240 g
2 cups chopped pecans	220 g

- Preheat oven to 350° (175° C).

- Beat brown sugar, eggs and biscuit mix in bowl.

- Stir in pecans and pour into sprayed 9 x 13-inch (23 x 33 cm) baking pan.

- Bake for 35 minutes, cool and cut into squares. Yields 12 squares.

Snicker Brownies

1 (18 ounce) box German chocolate cake mix	**510 g**
¾ cup (1½ sticks) butter, melted	**170 g**
½ cup evaporated milk	**125 ml**
4 (2.7 ounce) Snickers® candy bars, cut in	
⅛-inch (3 mm) slices	**4 (75 g)**

- Preheat oven to 350° (175° C).

- Combine cake mix, butter and evaporated milk in large bowl and beat on low speed until mixture blends well.

- Place half batter in sprayed, floured 9 x 13-inch (23 x 33 cm) baking pan and bake for 10 minutes.

- Remove from oven and place candy bar slices evenly over brownies.

- Drop spoonfuls of remaining over candy bars and spread as evenly as possible.

- Return to oven and bake for additional 20 minutes. When cool, cut into bars. Yields 12 squares.

■ ■

Brownies are really easy to make and are always a popular choice. About the only way you can really mess up brownies is to overcook them. Fudgy brownies are a little better if they are slightly undercooked. Cake brownies are best with frosting.

■ ■

Gooey Turtle Bars

½ cup (1 stick) butter, melted	115 g
2 cups vanilla wafer crumbs	320 g
1 (12 ounce) package semi-sweet chocolate chips	340 g
1 cup pecan pieces	110 g
1 (12 ounce) jar caramel ice cream topping	340 g

- Preheat oven to 350° (175° C).

- Combine butter and wafer crumbs in 9 x 13-inch (23 x 33 cm) baking pan and press into bottom of pan. Sprinkle with chocolate chips and pecans.

- Remove lid from caramel topping and microwave on HIGH for 30 seconds or until hot. Drizzle topping over pecans.

- Bake for about 15 minutes or until chocolate chips melt. (Make sure chocolate melts but crumbs don't burn.)

- Cool in pan and refrigerate for at least 30 minutes before cutting into squares. Yields 12 squares.

TIP: Watch bars closely – you want the chips to melt, but you don't want the crumbs to burn.

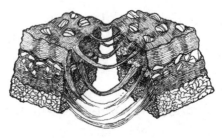

Apricot Bars

1¼ cups flour	150 g
¾ cup packed brown sugar	165 g
6 tablespoons (¾ stick) butter	85 g
¾ cup apricot preserves	240 g

- Preheat oven to 350° (175° C).

- Combine flour, brown sugar and butter in bowl and mix well.

- Place half mixture in sprayed 9-inch (23 cm) square baking pan, spread apricot preserves over top and sprinkle with remaining flour mixture. Bake for 30 minutes. Cut into squares. Yields 9 squares.

Walnut Bars

1⅔ cups graham cracker crumbs	175 g
1½ cups coarsely chopped walnuts	195 g
1 (14 ounce) can sweetened condensed milk	395 g
¼ cup flaked coconut, optional	20 g

- Preheat oven to 350° (175° C).

- Place graham cracker crumbs and walnuts in bowl. Slowly add sweetened condensed milk, coconut and a dash of salt. (Mixture will be very thick.)

- Pack into sprayed 9-inch (23 cm) square pan and press mixture down with back of spoon. Bake for 35 minutes and cut into squares when cool. Yields 9 squares.

Chinese Cookies

1 (6 ounce) package butterscotch chips	170 g
1 (6 ounce) package chocolate chips	170 g
2 cups chow mein noodles	110 g
1¼ cups salted peanuts	190 g

- Melt butterscotch and chocolate chips in saucepan on low heat. Add noodles and peanuts and mix well.

- Drop teaspoonfuls of mixture onto wax paper and refrigerate to harden.

- Store in airtight container. Yields 3 dozen cookies.

Butterscotch Cookies

1 (12 ounce) and 1 (6 ounce) package butterscotch chips	510 g
2¼ cups chow mein noodles	125 g
½ cup chopped walnuts	65 g
¼ cup flaked coconut	20 g

- Melt butterscotch chips in double boiler. Add noodles, walnuts and coconut.

- Drop tablespoonfuls of mixture onto wax paper. Yields 3 dozen cookies.

Coconut Yummies

1 (12 ounce) package white chocolate baking chips	340 g
¼ cup (½ stick) butter	60 g
16 large marshmallows	
2 cups quick-cooking oats	160 g
1 cup flaked coconut	85 g

- Melt chocolate chips, butter and marshmallows in saucepan over low heat and stir until smooth. Stir in oats and coconut and mix well.

- Drop rounded teaspoonfuls of mixture onto wax paper lined cookie sheets.

- Refrigerate until set and store in airtight container. Yields 3 dozen cookies.

Haystacks

1 (12 ounce) package butterscotch chips	340 g
1 cup salted peanuts	150 g
1½ cups chow mein noodles	85 g

- Melt butterscotch chips in double boiler. Remove from heat and stir in peanuts and noodles.

- Drop teaspoonfuls of mixture onto wax paper.

- Cool and store in airtight container. Yields 2 dozen cookies.

Orange Balls

1 (12 ounce) box vanilla wafers, crushed	340 g
½ cup (1 stick) butter, melted	115 g
1 (16 ounce) box powdered sugar	455 g
1 (6 ounce) can frozen orange juice concentrate, thawed	175 ml
1 cup finely chopped pecans	110 g

- Combine wafer crumbs, butter, powdered sugar and orange juice concentrate in bowl and mix well.

- Form into balls, roll in chopped pecans and store in airtight container.

- Make these in finger shapes for something different. They make neat cookies for a party or a tea. Yields 3 dozen balls.

Peanut Butter Crunchies

1 cup sugar	200 g
½ cup light corn syrup	125 ml
2 cups peanut butter	575 g
4 cups rice crispy cereal	105 g

- Combine sugar and syrup in saucepan and bring to a rolling boil.

- Remove from stove and stir in peanut butter. Add cereal and mix well.

- Drop teaspoonfuls of mixture onto wax paper and place in refrigerator for a few minutes to set. Yields 48 cookies.

Scotch Shortbread

½ cup (1 stick) unsalted butter, softened	115 g
⅓ cup sugar	65 g
1¼ cups flour	150 g
Powdered sugar	

- Preheat oven to 325° (165° C).

- Cream butter and sugar in bowl until light and fluffy. Add flour and a dash of salt and mix well.

- Spread dough into 8-inch (20 cm) square pan and bake for 20 minutes or until light brown. Let shortbread cool in pan, dust with powdered sugar and cut into squares. Yields 9 squares.

Sand Tarts

1 cup (2 sticks) butter, softened	230 g
¾ cup powdered sugar	90 g
2 cups flour	240 g
1 cup chopped pecans	110 g
1 teaspoon vanilla	5 ml

- Preheat oven to 325° (165° C). Cream butter and powdered sugar in bowl and add flour, pecans and vanilla.

- Roll into crescents and place on unsprayed cookie sheet. Bake for 20 minutes and roll in extra powdered sugar after tarts cool. Yields 3 dozen cookies.

Pecan Puffs

2 egg whites
¾ cup packed light brown sugar   **165 g**
1 teaspoon vanilla   **5 ml**
1 cup chopped pecans   **110 g**

- Preheat oven to 250° (120° C).

- Beat egg whites in bowl until foamy and add brown sugar ¼ cup (55 g) at a time and continue beating.

- Add vanilla, continue beating until stiff peaks form (about 3 or 4 minutes) and fold in pecans.

- Line cookie sheet with freezer paper and drop teaspoonsful of mixture onto paper.

- Bake for 45 minutes. Yields 3 dozen cookies.

Reuse those holiday tins. Once the cookies are all gone, use the colorful tins to store baking items and accessories, such as all those tools you used to decorate that cake – five years ago.

Coconut Macaroons

2 (7 ounce) packages flaked coconut	2 (200 g)
1 (14 ounce) can sweetened condensed milk	395 g
2 teaspoons vanilla	10 ml
½ teaspoon almond extract	2 ml

- Preheat oven to 350° (175° C).

- Combine coconut, sweetened condensed milk and extracts in bowl and mix well.

- Drop rounded teaspoonfuls of mixture onto foil-lined cookie sheet. Bake for 8 to 10 minutes or until light brown around edges.

- Immediately remove from foil. (Macaroons will stick if allowed to cool.) Store at room temperature. Yields 3 dozen cookies.

Butter Cookies

1 pound butter	455 g
¾ cup packed brown sugar	165 g
¾ cup sugar	150 g
4½ cups flour	540 g

- Preheat oven to 350° (175° C).

- Cream butter, brown sugar and sugar in bowl, slowly add flour and mix well. (Batter will be very thick.)

- Roll into small balls and place on unsprayed cookie sheet. Bake for about 15 minutes until only slightly brown. (Do not overbake.) Yields 3 dozen cookies.

Devil's Food Cookies

1 (18 ounce) box devil's food cake mix	510 g
½ cup canola oil	125 ml
2 eggs	
¾ cup chopped pecans, optional	85 g

- Preheat oven to 350° (175° C). Combine cake mix, oil and eggs in bowl and mix well. (If you like, fold in chopped pecans.)

- Drop teaspoonfuls of mixture onto non-stick cookie sheet.

- Bake for 10 to 12 minutes. Cool and remove to wire rack. Yields 3 dozen cookies.

Brown Sugar Cookies

¾ cup packed brown sugar	165 g
1 cup (2 sticks) butter, softened	230 g
1 egg yolk	
2 cups flour	240 g

- Cream sugar and butter in bowl until light and fluffy. Mix in egg yolk and blend in flour. Refrigerate dough for 1 hour.

- When ready to bake, preheat oven to 325° (165° C).

- Form dough into 1-inch (2.5 cm) balls; flatten and criss-cross with fork on lightly sprayed cookie sheet.

- Bake for 10 to 12 minutes or until golden brown. Yields 2 dozen cookies.

Cherry Crisp

2 (20 ounce) cans cherry pie filling	**2 (570 g)**
1 (18 ounce) box white cake mix	**510 g**
½ cup (1 stick) butter	**115 g**
2 cups chopped pecans	**220 g**

- Preheat oven to 350° (175° C).

- Pour pie filling into sprayed 9 x 13-inch (23 x 33 cm) baking dish. Sprinkle cake mix over top of filling.

- Dot with butter and cover with pecans. Bake uncovered for 45 minutes. Serves 8 to 10.

Blueberry Crunch

1 (20 ounce) can crushed pineapple with juice	**570 g**
1 (18 ounce) box yellow cake mix	**510 g**
3 cups fresh or frozen blueberries	**460 g**
⅔ cup sugar	**135 g**
½ cup (1 stick) butter, melted	**450 g**

- Preheat oven to 350° (175° C).

- Spread pineapple in sprayed 9 x 13-inch (23 x 33 cm) baking dish and sprinkle cake mix, blueberries and sugar.

- Drizzle with butter and bake for 45 minutes or until bubbly. Serves 8 to 10.

Apricot Cobbler

So easy and so good!

1 (20 ounce) can apricot pie filling	570 g
1 (20 ounce) can crushed pineapple with juice	570 g
1 cup chopped pecans	110 g
1 (18 ounce) box yellow cake mix	510 g
1 cup (2 sticks) butter, melted	230 g
Whipped topping, thawed	

- Preheat oven to 375° (190° C).

- Pour pie filling in sprayed 9 x 13-inch (23 x 33 cm) baking dish and spread.

- Spoon pineapple and juice over pie filling and sprinkle pecans over pineapple.

- Sprinkle cake mix over pecans.

- Drizzle melted butter over cake mix and bake for 40 minutes or until light brown and crunchy.

- Serve hot or room temperature. (It's great topped with whipped topping.) Serves 8 to 10.

Cherry Cobbler

2 (20 ounce) cans cherry pie filling   **2 (570 g)**
1 (18 ounce) box white cake mix   **510 g**
¾ cup (1½ sticks) butter, melted   **170 g**
1 (4 ounce) package slivered almonds   **115 g**
Whipped topping, thawed

- Preheat oven to 350° (175° C).

- Spread pie filling in sprayed 9 x 13-inch (23 x 33 cm) baking pan. Sprinkle cake mix over pie filling, drizzle with melted butter and sprinkle almonds over top.

- Bake for 45 minutes. Top with whipped topping. Serves 8 to 10.

Easy Pumpkin Pie

2 eggs
1 (30 ounce) can pumpkin   **810 g**
1 (5 ounce) can evaporated milk   **150 ml**
1 (9 inch) deep-dish piecrust   **23 cm**

- Preheat oven to 400° (205° C).

- Beat eggs lightly in large bowl and stir in pumpkin and evaporated milk. Pour into piecrust. (Cover piecrust edges with strips of foil to prevent excessive browning.)

- Bake for 15 minutes. Reduce oven to 325° (165° C) and bake for additional 40 minutes or until knife inserted in center comes out clean and cool. Serves 6 to 8.

Easy Chocolate Pie

1 (8 ounce) milk chocolate candy bar	230 g
1 (16 ounce) carton whipped topping, thawed, divided	455 g
¾ cup chopped pecans	85 g
1 (9 inch) piecrust, baked	23 cm

- Break candy into small pieces in saucepan and melt over low heat. Remove and cool several minutes.

- Fold in two-thirds whipped topping, mix well and stir in chopped pecans. Pour into piecrust, spread remaining whipped topping over top and refrigerate for at least 8 hours. Serves 6 to 8.

Dixie Pie

24 large marshmallows	
1 cup evaporated milk	250 ml
1 (8 ounce) carton whipping cream, whipped	250 ml
3 tablespoons bourbon	45 ml
1 (6 ounce) chocolate piecrust	170 g

- Melt marshmallows in milk in saucepan over low heat and stir constantly. (Do not boil.) Cool in refrigerator.

- Fold into whipped cream while adding bourbon and pour into piecrust. Refrigerate for at least 5 hours before serving. Serves 6.

Black Forest Pie

This is definitely a party dessert, but the family
will insist it should be served on a regular basis.

4 (1 ounce) squares unsweetened baking chocolate	**4 (30 g)**
1 (14 ounce) can sweetened condensed milk	**395 g**
1 teaspoon almond extract	**5 ml**
1½ cups whipping cream, whipped	**375 ml**
1 (9 inch) piecrust, baked	**23 cm**
1 (20 ounce) can cherry pie filling, chilled	**570 g**

- Melt chocolate with sweetened condensed milk in saucepan over medium-low heat and stir well to mix.

- Remove from heat and stir in almond extract. Let mixture cool.

- When mixture is about room temperature, pour chocolate into whipped cream and fold gently until they combine.

- Pour into piecrust.

- To serve, spoon heaping spoonful of cherry filling over each piece of pie. Serves 6 to 8.

Do not keep chocolate in the refrigerator. It is best
when stored between 60° and 70° F (16° - 21° C).

Chess Pie

½ cup (1 stick) butter, softened	115 g
2 cups sugar	400 g
1 tablespoon cornstarch	15 ml
4 eggs	
1 (9 inch) piecrust	23 cm

- Preheat oven to 325° (165° C). Cream butter, sugar and cornstarch in bowl. Add eggs one at a time and beat well after each addition.

- Pour mixture into piecrust. (Cover piecrust edges with strips of foil to prevent excessive browning.)

- Bake for 45 minutes or until center sets. Serves 6 to 8.

Peanut Butter Pie

⅔ cup crunchy peanut butter	190 g
1 (8 ounce) package cream cheese, softened	230 g
½ cup milk	125 ml
1 cup powdered sugar	120 g
1 (8 ounce) carton whipped topping, thawed	250 ml
1 (9 ounce) graham cracker piecrust	255 g

- Beat peanut butter, cream cheese, milk and powdered sugar in bowl and fold in whipped topping.

- Pour into piecrust and refrigerate for several hours before serving. Serves 6.

Creamy Lemon Pie

1 (8 ounce) package cream cheese, softened	230 g
1 (14 ounce) can sweetened condensed milk	395 g
¼ cup lemon juice	60 ml
1 (20 ounce) can lemon pie filling	570 g
1 (9 ounce) graham cracker piecrust	255 g

- Beat cream cheese in bowl until creamy.

- Add sweetened condensed milk and lemon juice and beat until mixture is very creamy.

- Fold in lemon pie filling, stir until creamy and pour into piecrust.

- Refrigerate for several hours before slicing and serving. Serves 6.

Limeade Pie

1 (6 ounce) can frozen limeade concentrate, thawed	175 ml
2 cups low-fat frozen yogurt, softened	400 g
1 (8 ounce) carton whipped topping, thawed	230 g
1 (6 ounce) graham cracker piecrust	170 g

- Combine limeade concentrate and yogurt in bowl and mix well.

- Fold in whipped topping and pour into piecrust.

- Freeze for at least 4 hours or overnight. Serves 6.

Peach-Mousse Pie

Incredibly good!

1 (16 ounce) package frozen peach slices, thawed	455 g
1 cup sugar	200 g
1 (1 ounce) packet unflavored gelatin	30 g
⅛ teaspoon ground nutmeg	.5 ml
¾ (8 ounce) carton whipped topping, thawed	¾ (230 g)
1 (9 ounce) graham cracker piecrust	255 g

- Place peaches in blender and process until smooth.

- Transfer peaches to saucepan, bring to a boil and stir constantly.

- Combine sugar, gelatin and nutmeg in bowl and stir into hot puree until sugar and gelatin dissolve.

- Pour gelatin-peach mixture into large bowl.

- Place in freezer until mixture mounds (about 20 minutes) and stir occasionally

- Beat mixture on high speed for about 5 minutes until it becomes light and frothy.

- Fold in whipped topping and spoon into piecrust. Serves 6.

Strawberry-Cream Cheese Pie

2 (10 ounce) packages frozen sweetened	
strawberries, thawed	**2 (280 g)**
2 (8 ounce) packages cream cheese, softened	**2 (230 g)**
⅔ cup powdered sugar	**80 g**
1 (8 ounce) carton whipped topping, thawed	**230 g**
1 (6 ounce) chocolate piecrust	**170 g**
Fresh strawberries	

- Drain strawberries and set aside ¼ cup (60 ml) juice.

- Combine cream cheese, reserved juice, strawberries and powdered sugar in bowl and beat well.

- Fold in whipped topping and spoon into piecrust.

- Refrigerate overnight and garnish with fresh strawberries. Serves 6.

When you need a dessert in a hurry, buy a cheesecake and pour a can of cherry pie filling over the top.

Easy Cheesecake

2 (8 ounce) packages cream cheese, softened	**2 (230 g)**
½ cup sugar	**100 g**
½ teaspoon vanilla	**2 ml**
2 eggs	
1 (9 ounce) graham cracker piecrust	**255 g**
Pie filling, any flavor	

- Preheat oven to 350° (175° C).

- Beat cream cheese, sugar, vanilla and eggs in bowl and pour into piecrust.

- Bake for 40 minutes.

- Cool and top with any flavor pie filling. Serves 6.

Old-Fashioned Applesauce Spice Cake

1 (18 ounce) box spice cake mix	510 g
3 eggs	
1¼ cups applesauce	320 g
⅓ cup canola oil	75 ml
1 cup chopped pecans	110 g
1 (16 ounce) can vanilla frosting	455 g
½ teaspoon cinnamon	2 ml

- Preheat oven to 350° (175° C).

- Combine cake mix, eggs, applesauce and oil and beat on medium speed for 2 minutes.

- Stir in pecans and pour into sprayed, floured 9 x 13-inch (23 x 33 cm) baking pan.

- Bake for 40 minutes or until toothpick inserted near center comes out clean. Cool.

- For frosting, stir vanilla frosting and cinnamon together. Serves 8 to 10.

Lemon-Pineapple Cake

1 (18 ounce) box lemon cake mix	**510 g**
1 (20 ounce) can crushed pineapple with juice	**570 g**
3 eggs	
⅓ cup canola oil	**75 ml**

- Preheat oven to 350° (175° C).

- Combine cake mix, pineapple, eggs and oil in bowl. Blend on low speed to moisten and beat on medium for 2 minutes.

- Pour batter into sprayed, floured 9 x 13-inch (23 x 33 cm) baking pan.

- Bake for 30 minutes. Cake is done when toothpick inserted in center comes out clean. (While cake is baking, prepare topping.) Cool for 15 minutes.

Lemon-Pineapple Cake Topping:

1 (14 ounce) can sweetened condensed milk	**395 g**
1 cup sour cream	**240 g**
¼ cup lemon juice	**60 ml**

- Combine all topping ingredients in medium bowl. Stir well to blend.

- Pour over warm cake. Refrigerate. Serves 8 to 10.

Hawaiian Dream Cake

This looks like a lot of trouble to make, but it really isn't. And it is a wonderful cake!

1 (18 ounce) box yellow cake mix	**510 g**
4 eggs	
¾ cup canola oil	**175 ml**
½ (20 ounce) can crushed pineapple with half juice	**½ (570 g)**

- Preheat oven to 350° (175° C).

- Beat cake mix, eggs, oil and pineapple in bowl for 4 minutes. Pour into sprayed, floured 9 x 13-inch (23 x 33 cm) baking pan.

- Bake for 30 to 35 minutes or until toothpick inserted in centers comes out clean. Cool and spread Coconut-Pineapple topping over cake.

Coconut-Pineapple Topping:

½ (20 ounce) can crushed pineapple with half juice	**½ (570 g)**
½ cup (1 stick) butter	**115 g**
1 (16 ounce) box powdered sugar	**455 g**
1 (6 ounce) can flaked coconut	**170 g**

- Heat pineapple and butter in saucepan and boil for 2 minutes. Add powdered sugar and coconut.

- Punch holes in cake with knife and pour hot topping over cake. Serves 8 to 10.

Two-Surprise Cake

*The first surprise is how easy it is and the second surprise
is how good it is! You'll make this more than once.*

1 bakery orange-chiffon cake	
1 (15 ounce) can crushed pineapple with juice	**425 g**
1 (3.4 ounce) package instant vanilla pudding mix	**95 g**
1 (8 ounce) carton whipped topping, thawed	**230 g**
½ cup slivered almonds, toasted	**85 g**

- Slice cake horizontally into 3 equal layers.

- Mix pineapple, pudding mix and whipped topping in bowl and blend well.

- Spread pineapple mixture onto each cake layer and top of cake. Sprinkle almonds on top and refrigerate. Serves 18.

Strawberry Pound Cake

1 (18 ounce) box strawberry cake mix	**510 g**
1 (3.4 ounce) package instant pineapple pudding mix	**95 g**
⅓ cup canola oil	**75 ml**
4 eggs	
1 (3 ounce) package strawberry gelatin	**85 g**

- Preheat oven to 325° (165° C).

- Mix all ingredients plus 1 cup (250 ml) water in bowl and beat for 2 minutes on medium speed.

- Pour into sprayed, floured bundt pan.

- Bake for 55 to 60 minutes. Cake is done when toothpick inserted near center comes out clean.

- Cool for 20 minutes before removing cake from pan. If you would like a frosting, use a can of vanilla frosting. Serves 18 to 20.

TIP: *If you like coconut better than pineapple, use coconut cream pudding mix instead of pineapple.*

Sometimes the simplest of ideas makes the best dessert.
If you're hungry for something sweet or have unexpected
guests, you can't go wrong with a can of pie filling poured
over a ready-made cake and topped with whipped topping.

Coconut Cake Deluxe

This is a fabulous cake!

1 (18 ounce) box yellow cake mix	**510 g**
1 (14 ounce) can sweetened condensed milk	**395 g**
1 (15 ounce) can coconut cream	**445 ml**
1 (3 ounce) can flaked coconut	**85 g**
1 (8 ounce) carton whipped topping, thawed	**230 g**

- Preheat oven to 350° (175° C).

- Mix cake batter according to package directions.

- Pour batter into sprayed, floured 9 x 13-inch (23 x 33 cm) baking pan and bake for 30 to 35 minutes or until toothpick inserted in center comes out clean.

- While cake is warm, punch holes in cake about 2 inches (5 cm) apart. (A straw is convenient for punching holes.)

- Pour sweetened condensed milk over cake and spread until all milk soaks into cake.

- Pour coconut cream over cake and sprinkle with coconut.

- Cool, frost with whipped topping and refrigerate. Serves 8 to 10.

Oreo Cake

1 (18 ounce) box white cake mix	**510 g**
⅓ cup canola oil	**75 ml**
4 egg whites	
1¼ cup coarsely chopped Oreo® cookies	
(about 11 cookies)	**125 g**

- Preheat oven to 350° (175° C). Combine cake mix, oil, egg whites and 1¼ cups (310 ml) water in bowl.

- Mix on low speed until moist and then beat for 2 minutes on high speed. Gently fold in coarsely chopped cookies and pour batter into 2 sprayed, floured 8-inch (20 cm) round cake pans.

- Bake for 25 to 30 minutes or until toothpick inserted in center comes out clean. Cool for 15 minutes and remove from pan. Cool completely and frost.

Oreo Cake Frosting:

4¼ cups powdered sugar	**510 g**
1 cup (2 sticks) butter, softened	**230 g**
1 cup shortening (do NOT use butter-flavored	
shortening)	**190 g**
1 teaspoon almond extract	**5 ml**
½ cup crushed Oreo® cookies (about 4 - 5 cookies)	**50 g**

- Combine all frosting ingredients in bowl and beat until creamy. Frost first layer of cake, place second layer on top and frost top and sides. Sprinkle cookie crumbs over top. Serves 18.

Chocolate-Cherry Cake

This is a chocolate lover's dream.

1 (18 ounce) box milk chocolate cake mix	510 g
1 (20 ounce) can cherry pie filling	570 g
3 eggs	

- Preheat oven to 350° (175° C).

- Combine cake mix, pie filling and eggs in bowl.

- Mix with spoon and pour into sprayed, floured 9 x 13-inch (23 x 33 cm) baking dish.

- Bake for 35 to 40 minutes. Cake is done when toothpick inserted in center comes out clean.

Chocolate-Cherry Cake Frosting:

5 tablespoons (⅔ stick) butter	70 g
1¼ cups sugar	250 g
½ cup milk	125 ml
1 (6 ounce) package chocolate chips	170 g

- When cake is done, combine butter, sugar and milk in medium saucepan.

- Boil for 1 minute and stir constantly.

- Add chocolate chips and stir until chips melt.

- Pour over hot cake. Serves 8 to 10.

Twinkie Dessert

1 (15 ounce) box Twinkies® (10 count)	**425 g**
4 bananas, sliced	
1 (5 ounce) package instant vanilla pudding mix	**145 g**
1 (20 ounce) can crushed pineapple, drained	**570 g**
1 (8 ounce) carton whipped topping, thawed	**230 g**

- Slice Twinkies® in half lengthwise and place in sprayed 9 x 13-inch (23 x 33 cm) pan cream-side up.

- Layer sliced bananas over Twinkies®.

- Prepare pudding according to package directions (use 2 cups/500 ml milk).

- Pour pudding over bananas and add pineapple.

- Top with whipped topping and refrigerate.

- Cut into squares to serve. Serves 6 to 8.

Strawberry Trifle

1 (5 ounce) package instant French vanilla pudding mix   145 g
1 (12 ounce) bakery pound cake, sliced,
    divided   340 g
½ cup sherry, divided   125 ml
2 cups fresh strawberries, sliced, divided   330 g
Whipped topping, thawed

- Prepare pudding according to package directions.

- Layer half pound cake slices in 8-inch (20 cm) crystal bowl and sprinkle with half sherry.

- Layer half strawberries and half pudding on top.

- Repeat all layers and refrigerate overnight or for several hours.

- Before serving, top with whipped topping. Serves 8 to 10.

Peachy Sundaes

1 pint vanilla ice cream   475 ml
¾ cup peach preserves, warmed   240 g
¼ cup chopped almonds, toasted   40 g
¼ cup flaked coconut   20 g

- Divide ice cream into 4 sherbet dishes.

- Top with preserves.

- Sprinkle with almonds and coconut. Serves 4.

Mango Cream

2 soft mangoes
½ gallon vanilla ice cream, softened   **945 ml**
1 (6 ounce) can frozen lemonade concentrate, thawed   **175 ml**
1 (8 ounce) carton whipped topping, thawed   **230 g**

- Peel mangoes, cut slices around seeds and cut into small chunks.

- Combine ice cream, lemonade concentrate and whipped topping in large bowl and fold in mango chunks.

- Quickly spoon mixture into parfait or sherbet glasses and cover with plastic wrap. Freeze. Serves 8.

Butterscotch Finale

1 (16 ounce) carton whipping cream	500 ml
¾ cup butterscotch ice cream topping	215 g
1 (14 ounce) bakery angel food cake	395 g
¾ pound toffee bars, crushed, divided	340 g

- Whip cream in bowl until thick.

- Slowly add butterscotch topping and continue to beat until mixture is thick.

- Slice cake horizontally into 3 equal layers.

- Place bottom layer on cake plate, spread with 1½ cups (375 ml) whipped cream mixture and sprinkle with one-fourth crushed toffee.

- Repeat layers and frost top and sides of cake with remaining whipped cream mixture.

- Sprinkle remaining toffee over top of cake. Refrigerate for at least 8 hours before serving. Serves 15.

Keeping an angel food cake in the freezer will make you look like a kitchen pro when it comes time to prepare a last-minute dessert. You can top the cake with fresh berries, pie filling, ice cream, chocolate syrup, butterscotch topping, or caramel sauce and – always – whipped topping.

Ice Cream Dessert

19 ice cream sandwiches
1 (12 ounce) carton whipped topping, thawed   340 g
1 (12 ounce) jar hot fudge ice cream topping   340 g
1 cup salted peanuts   150 g

- Cut 1 ice cream sandwich in half.

- Place 1 whole and 1 half sandwich along short side of unsprayed 9 x 13-inch (23 x 33 cm) pan.

- Arrange 8 sandwiches in opposite direction in pan.

- Spread with half whipped topping.

- Spoon teaspoonfuls of fudge topping onto whipped topping and sprinkle with half peanuts.

- Repeat layers with remaining ice cream sandwiches, whipped topping and peanuts. (Pan will be full.)

- Cover and freeze. Take out of freezer 20 minutes before cutting into squares and serving. Serves 6 to 8.

Blueberry-Angel Dessert

1 (8 ounce) package cream cheese, softened	230 g
1 cup powdered sugar	120 g
1 (8 ounce) carton whipped topping, thawed	230 g
1 (14 ounce) bakery angel food cake	395 g
2 (20 ounce) cans blueberry pie filling	2 (570 g)

- Beat cream cheese and powdered sugar in large bowl and fold in whipped topping.

- Tear cake into small 1 or 2-inch (1.2 or 2.5 cm) cubes and fold into cream cheese mixture.

- Spread mixture evenly in 9 x 13-inch (23 x 33 cm) dish and top with pie filling.

- Cover and refrigerate for at least 3 hours before cutting into squares to serve. Serves 6 to 8.

When you need a dessert fast, try ice cream with liqueur poured over it. Keep on hand a bottle of almond-flavored liqueur (amaretto), coffee-flavored liqueur (Kahlua®), and your favorite fruit-flavored liqueur. It's so fast and easy! And it tastes really special.

Blueberry Fluff

1 (20 ounce) can blueberry pie filling	**570 g**
1 (20 ounce) can crushed pineapple, drained	**570 g**
1 (14 ounce) can sweetened condensed milk	**395 g**
1 (8 ounce) carton whipped topping, thawed	**230 g**

- Mix pie filling, pineapple and sweetened condensed milk in bowl.

- Fold in whipped topping. (This dessert is even better if you add ¾ cup/85 g chopped pecans.)

- Pour into parfait glasses and refrigerate. Serves 8.

Brandied Fruit

2 (20 ounce) cans crushed pineapple	**2 (570 g)**
1 (16 ounce) can sliced peaches	**455 g**
2 (11 ounce) cans mandarin oranges	**2 (310 g)**
1 (10 ounce) jar maraschino cherries	**280 g**
Sugar	
1 cup brandy	**250 ml**

- Let all fruit drain for 12 hours in refrigerator.

- For every cup (250 ml) of drained fruit, add ½ cup (100 g) sugar. Let stand for 12 hours.

- Add brandy, spoon into large jar and store in refrigerator. This mixture needs to stand in refrigerator for 3 weeks.

- Serve over ice cream. Yields 2 quarts (2 L).

Fun Fruit Fajitas

1 (20 ounce) can cherry pie filling	570 g
8 large flour tortillas	
1½ cups sugar	300 g
¾ cup (1½ sticks) butter	170 g
1 teaspoon almond extract	5 ml

- Divide pie filling equally on tortillas, roll and place in 9 x 13-inch (23 x 33 cm) baking dish.

- Mix sugar and butter in saucepan with 2 cups (500 ml) water and bring to a boil.

- Add almond extract and pour sugar mixture over flour tortillas.

- Place in refrigerator and soak for 1 to 24 hours.

- When ready to bake, preheat oven to 350° (175° C).

- Bake for 20 minutes or until brown and bubbly. Serve hot or at room temperature. Serves 6 to 8.

TIP: Use any flavor of pie filling you like.

Amaretto Peaches

4½ cups peeled, sliced fresh peaches	655 g
½ cup amaretto liqueur	125 ml
½ cup sour cream	120 g
½ cup packed brown sugar	110 g

- Lay peaches in 2-quart (2 L) baking dish.

- Pour amaretto over peaches and spread with sour cream.

- Sprinkle brown sugar evenly over top.

- Broil mixture until it heats thoroughly and sugar melts.

- Serve over ice cream or pound cake. Serves 6.

Amaretto Ice Cream

1 (8 ounce) carton whipping cream, whipped	250 ml
1 pint vanilla ice cream, softened	475 ml
⅓ cup amaretto liqueur	75 ml
⅓ cup chopped almonds, toasted	55 g

- Combine whipped cream, ice cream and amaretto and freeze in sherbet glasses.

- When ready to serve, drizzle a little additional amaretto over top of each individual serving and sprinkle with toasted almonds. Serves 6.

APPENDICES

U.S. and Metric Measurements

Please note: In U.S. cookery, all ingredients are measured by volume. In metric measurements, dry ingredients plus some other items are measured by weight (grams and kilograms), not by volume (milliliters and liters).

Common Metric Abbreviations:

Grams	g
Kilograms	kg
Milliliters	ml
Liters	L
Millimeters	mm
Centimeters	cm

Basic Conversion Formulas

1 fluid ounce = 29.57 milliliters

1 avoirdupois ounce (weight) = 28.35 grams

continued next page...

U.S. and Metric Measurements — continued

Liquid Volume

3 teaspoons	1 tablespoon	0.5 fluid ounce	15 ml
4 tablespoons	¼ cup	2 fluid ounces	60 ml
8 tablespoons	½ cup	4 fluid ounces	125 ml
12 tablespoons	¾ cup	6 fluid ounces	175 ml
16 tablespoons	1 cup	8 fluid ounces	250 ml
¼ cup	4 tablespoons	2 fluid ounces	60 ml
⅓ cup	5 tablespoons + 1 teaspoon	2.7 fluid ounces	75 ml
½ cup	8 tablespoons	4 fluid ounces	125 ml
⅔ cup	10 tablespoons + 2 teaspoons	5.4 fluid ounces	150 ml
¾ cup	12 tablespoons	6 fluid ounces	175 ml
1 cup	16 tablespoons; ½ pint	8 fluid ounces	250 ml
2 cups	1 pint	16 fluid ounces	
3 cups	1½ pints	24 fluid ounces	
4 cups	1 quart	32 fluid ounces	
8 cups	2 quarts	64 fluid ounces	
1 pint	2 cups	16 fluid ounces	
2 pints	1 quart	32 fluid ounces	
1 quart	2 pints; 4 cups	32 fluid ounces	
4 quarts	1 gallon; 8 pints; 16 cups	64 fluid ounces	

Other Volume Measures

8 quarts . . . . 1 peck

4 pecks. . . . . 1 bushel

continued next page...

U.S. and Metric Measurements — continued

Weight Measurements

Avoirdupois Ounces	Pounds	Metric (grams)
1 ounce		30 grams
2 ounces		55 grams
3 ounces		85 grams
4 ounces	¼ pound	115 grams
5 ounces		140 grams
6 ounces		170 grams
8 ounces	½ pound	230 grams
10 ounces		280 grams
12 ounces	¼ pound	340 grams
14 ounces		395 grams
16 ounces	1 pound	455 grams
32 ounces	2 pounds	910 grams
35 ounces	2.2 pounds	1 kilogram

Distance (Length) Measurements

Inches	Centimeters
0.39 inch	1 cm
1 inch	2.54 cm
12 inches (1 foot(	30.48 cm
36 inches (3 feet)	91.44 cm
39.37 inches	1 meter (100 cm)

Common Pan and Casserole Sizes and Volumes

U.S. Measurements		Metric Measurements	
Round	**Volume**	**Round**	**Volume**
6 x 2	4 cups	15 x 5 cm	948 ml
8 x 1½	4 cups	20 x 4 cm	948 ml
8 x 2	6 cups	20 x 5 cm	1.4 L
9 x 1½	6 cups	23 x 4 cm	1.4 L
9 x 2	8 cups	23 x 5 cm	1.9 L
10 x 2	11 cups	25 x 5 cm	2.6 L
Springform	**Volume**	**Springform**	**Volume**
9 x 2½	10 cups		
8 x 3	11 cups	23 x 6 cm	2.4 L
9 x 3	12 cups	23 x 8 cm	2.8 L
10 x 2½	12 cups	25 x 6 cm	2.8 L
Bundt*	**Volume**	**Bundt**	**Volume**
7½ x 3	6 cups	19 x 8 cm	1.4 L
9 x 3	9 cups	23 x 8 cm	2.1 L
10 x 3½	12 cups	25 x 9 cm	2.8 L
10 x 3¾	12 cups		

* Bundt pans are known only in North America. They were created by NordicWare in 1950. The nearest European equivalent is a kugelhopf pan.

continued next page...

Common Pan and Casserole Sizes and Volumes — continued

U.S. Measurements		Metric Measurements	
Tube	**Volume**	**Tube**	**Volume**
8 x 3	9 cups	20 x 8 cm	2.1 L
9 x 3	12 cups	23 x 8 cm	2.8 L
9½ x 4	16 cups		
10 x 4	16 cups	25 x 10 cm	3.8 L
Square	**Volume**	**Square**	**Volume**
8 x 8 x 1½	6 cups	20 x 20 x 4 cm	1.4 L
8 x 8 x 2	8 cups	20 x 20 x 5 cm	1.9 L
9 x 9 x 1½	8 cups	23 x 23 x 4 cm	1.9 L
9 x 9 x 2	10 cups	23 x 23 x 5 cm	2.4 L
10 x 10 x 2	12 cups	25 x 25 x 5 cm	2.8 L
Rectangular	**Volume**	**Rectangular**	**Volume**
11 x 7 x 2	6 cups	28 x 18 x 5 cm	1.4 L
13 x 9 x 2	14 cups	33 x 23 x 5 cm	3.3 L
Loaf	**Volume**	**Loaf**	**Volume**
8 x 4 x 2½.	4 cups	20 x 10 x 6 cm	948 ml
8½ x 4½ x 2½	6 cups	21 x 11 x 6 cm	1.4 L
9 x 5 x 3	8 cups	23 x 13 x 8 cm	1.9 L
Muffin Cup	**Volume**	**Muffin Cup**	**Volume**
1¾ x ¾	⅛ cup	4.5 x 2 cm	30 ml
2¾ x 1⅛	¼ cup	7 x 3 cm	60 ml
2¾ x 1½	½ cup	7 x 4 cm	120 ml
3 x 1¼	⅝ cup	8 x 3 cm	150 ml

continued next page...

Common Pan and Casserole Sizes and Volumes — continued

U.S. Measurements		Metric Measurements	
Heart Shaped	**Volume**	**Heart Shaped**	**Volume**
8 x 2½	8 cups	20 x 6 cm	1.9 L
Pie	**Volume**		
8 x 1½	4 cups		
9 x 1½	5 cups		
9 x 2	8 cups		
10 x 1½	6 cups		
Tart	**Volume**		
11 x 1	4 cups		
Casserole	**Volume**		**Volume**
1 quart	4 cups		948 ml
1½ quarts	6 cups		1.4 L
2 quarts	8 cups		1.9 L
2½ quarts	10 cups		2.4 L
3 quarts	12 cups		2.8 L
4 quarts	16 cups		3.8 L
Jelly Roll/Sheet Pan	**Volume**	**Jelly Roll/Sheet Pan**	**Volume**
10½ x 15½ x 1	10 cups	27 x 39 x 2.5 cm	2.4 L
12½ x 17½ x 1	12 cups	32 x 44 x 2.5 cm	2.8 L

Food Substitutions

You Need:	Use Instead:
1 cup breadcrumbs	¾ cup cracker crumbs
1 cup butter	⅞ cup vegetable oil or shortening
1 cup buttermilk	1 cup milk plus 1 tablespoon vinegar or lemon juice; or 1 cup plain yogurt
1 ounce unsweetened chocolate	3 tablespoons unsweetened cocoa plus 1 tablespoon butter
1 tablespoon cornstarch	2 tablespoons flour
1 cup cracker crumbs	1¼ cups breadcrumbs
1 cup cake flour	1 cup, less 2 tablespoons flour
1 clove garlic	1 teaspoon garlic salt less ½ teaspoon salt in recipe
1 tablespoon fresh herbs	1 teaspoon dried herbs
1 cup whole milk	½ cup evaporated milk plus ½ cup water; or ¾ cup nonfat milk plus ¼ cup butter
1 tablespoon prepared mustard	1 teaspoon dry mustard
1 small onion	1 tablespoon minced onion; or ½ teaspoon onion powder
1 cup sour cream	1 cup plain yogurt; or 1 tablespoon lemon juice plus enough evaporated whole milk to equal 1 cup
1 cup sugar	1¾ cups powdered sugar; or 1 cup packed brown sugar
1 cup powdered sugar	½ cup plus 1 tablespoon granulated sugar
1 cup tomato juice	½ cup tomato sauce plus ½ cup water
1 cup tomato sauce	½ cup tomato paste plus ½ cup water
1 cup yogurt	1 cup milk plus 1 tablespoon lemon juice

Pantry Basics

Most folks will not begin to want every item on the Grocery Checklist, but it will help you decide what to keep on hand for easy meals and ordinary needs.

You may also want to keep about a 3 to 4 day supply of bottled water and food that does not need to be cooked for emergencies. You can rotate this supply into your regular pantry so that items do not pass their expiration dates.

Convenience foods are great to have when you're in a hurry to get something on the table. You can even make your own "instant" meals and freeze or refrigerate for later use.

Here are some suggestions for basics to keep in your pantry:

Canned Savory Foods

Keep a supply of whole and chopped tomatoes; beans; vegetables such as corn, asparagus, and artichoke hearts; tuna; cooked ham; sauces; condensed and ready-to–heat soups; peanut and other nut butters.

continued next page…

Pantry Basics — continued

Canned Sweet Foods

Store canned fruits such as pineapple (chunks and slices); pears; peach halves or slices; exotic fruits such as litchis and guavas; fruit pie fillings; applesauce; and fruit cocktail.

Dry Foods and Packaged Mixes

Stock sauce and gravy mixes; dried vegetables; instant mashed potatoes; pasta and rice mixes; instant desserts; instant nonfat dry milk and gelatin powder; bread, pastry, batter, and cake mixes.

Bottled Foods and Preserves

Keep jams and jellies; fruits in brandy; ready-made meals such as chili or baked beans; pesto; olives; sun-dried tomatoes; and antipasto.

Prepared Foods

Stock up with partly baked breads and pastries; prepared ready-to-serve meals and pasta dishes; milk, cream, and whipped desserts.

continued next page...

Pantry Basics — continued

Refrigerated Foods

Refrigerated prepared meals; fresh pasta; soups; sweet and savory sauces; fruit salad; prepared mixed salads and dressings; fresh pastry; and dips.

Frozen Savory Foods

Frozen vegetables and stir-fry mixes; French fries; cooked rice; pizza bases; prepared fish and shellfish; meat and poultry; pastry, pies, and quiches.

Frozen Sweet Foods

Frozen prepared fruits, especially raspberries and seasonal soft-fruit mixes; melon balls; ices, sorbets, and iced desserts; cakes; and fruit juices.

Grocery Checklist

General Merchandise

Automotive

☐ _____
☐ _____
☐ _____

Baby Items

☐ _____
☐ _____
☐ _____

Cleaning supplies

☐ Dish Soap
☐ _____
☐ _____
☐ _____

Laundry

☐ Bleach
☐ Fabric Softener
☐ Laundry Detergent
☐ _____

Hardware

☐ _____
☐ _____
☐ _____

Paper Products

☐ Bath Tissue
☐ Facial Tissue
☐ Napkins
☐ Paper/Plastic Cups
☐ Paper Plates
☐ Paper Towels
☐ Plastic flatware
☐ _____

☐ _____

☐ _____

Pharmacy

☐ First aid

☐ OTC Medicine

☐ Prescriptions

☐ Toothpaste

☐ Vitamins

☐ _____

☐ _____

☐ _____

Toiletries

☐ Bath Soap

☐ Cosmetics

☐ Deodorant

☐ Lotion

☐ Shampoo

☐ _____

☐ _____

☐ _____

Miscellaneous General Merchandise

☐ Feminine Products

☐ Foil

☐ Plastic wrap

☐ Resealable bags

☐ Trash bags

☐ Greeting Cards

☐ Insecticides

☐ Light Bulbs

☐ Pet Supplies

☐ _____

☐ _____

☐ _____

☐ _____

☐ _____

☐ _____

☐ _____

Grocery Staples

Baking Supplies

- [ ] Almond bark (white, dark)
- [ ] Baking powder
- [ ] Baking soda
- [ ] Cake and cookie decorations (sprinkles, etc.)
- [ ] Chocolate (chips, squares)
  - [ ] butterscotch
  - [ ] milk chocolate
  - [ ] semisweet chocolate
  - [ ] unsweetened chocolate
  - [ ] white chocolate
- [ ] Cocoa, unsweetened
- [ ] Coconut, flaked
- [ ] Coconut cream
- [ ] Coconut milk
- [ ] Cooking spray
- [ ] Cornmeal (white, yellow)
- [ ] Cornstarch
- [ ] Corn syrup (light, dark)
- [ ] Cream of tartar
- [ ] Evaporated milk

- [ ] Flour
  - [ ] all-purpose
  - [ ] cake
  - [ ] quick-mixing (for gravies and sauces)
  - [ ] self-rising
  - [ ] unbleached
  - [ ] whole wheat)
- [ ] Food coloring
- [ ] Frostings
- [ ] Instant nonfat dry milk
- [ ] Marshmallows (large, miniature, marshmallow creme)
- [ ] Mixes
  - [ ] Biscuit or baking
  - [ ] Cake
  - [ ] Cornbread
  - [ ] Brownie
  - [ ] Muffin)
- [ ] Molasses
- [ ] Nuts
  - [ ] Almonds
  - [ ] Cashews
  - [ ] Hazelnuts
  - [ ] Peanuts

- [ ] Pecans
- [ ] Pine nuts (pignolias)
- [ ] Pistachios
- [ ] Walnuts)
- [ ] Oils
  - [ ] Asian sesame
  - [ ] Canola
  - [ ] Olive oil
  - [ ] Peanut
  - [ ] Safflower
- [ ] Piecrusts (chocolate, graham cracker)
- [ ] Seeds (pumpkin, sunflower)
- [ ] Shortening
- [ ] Sugar
  - [ ] Brown (light and dark)
  - [ ] Coarse (for decoration)
  - [ ] Granulated
  - [ ] Powdered
  - [ ] Superfine)
- [ ] Sweetened condensed milk
- [ ] Yeast, dry active (packets or cakes)
- [ ] _____

- [ ] _____
- [ ] _____
- [ ] _____

Beverages

- [ ] Beer
- [ ] Coffee (beans, ground, espresso, flavored, instant)
- [ ] Herbal teas
- [ ] Liqueurs (amaretto, creme de cacao, creme de menthe, Kahlua®, triple sec)
- [ ] Liquor (bourbon. brandy, gin, rum, whiskey)
- [ ] Soft drink mix (dry)
- [ ] Soft drinks (club soda, cola, lemon-lime, ginger ale)
- [ ] Teas (black, flavored, orange pekoe)
- [ ] Water
- [ ] Wine (champagne, red, rose, sherry, white)

- [ ] _____
- [ ] _____
- [ ] _____

Canned Fruits

- [ ] Applesauce
- [ ] Apricots
- [ ] Cherries (tart, sweet)
- [ ] Fruit cocktail
- [ ] Grapefruit
- [ ] Mandarin oranges
- [ ] Mangoes
- [ ] Maraschino cherries
- [ ] Mixed fruit
- [ ] Peaches (halves, sliced)
- [ ] Pears (halves, sliced)
- [ ] Pie apples
- [ ] Pie fillings
  - [ ] Apple
  - [ ] Apricot
  - [ ] Blackberry
  - [ ] Blueberry
  - [ ] Cherry
  - [ ] Lemon
  - [ ] Peach
  - [ ] Pineapple
  - [ ] Pumpkin)

- [ ] Pineapple (chunks, crushed, slices, tidbits)
- [ ] _____
- [ ] _____
- [ ] _____

Canned Juices

- [ ] Cranberry
- [ ] Grape
- [ ] Lemon
- [ ] Orange
- [ ] Pineapple
- [ ] Tomato
- [ ] _____
- [ ] _____
- [ ] _____

Canned Meats

- [ ] Anchovies
- [ ] Beef (dried, roast)
- [ ] Chicken
- [ ] Clams (chopped or whole baby)
- [ ] Crabmeat

- [ ] Deviled ham
- [ ] Dried beef
- [ ] Oysters
- [ ] Salmon
- [ ] Shrimp
- [ ] Tuna
- [ ] Turkey
- [ ] _____
- [ ] _____
- [ ] _____

Canned Soups

- [ ] Broths (chicken, beef, veggie)
- [ ] Cheddar cheese soup
- [ ] Cream of celery
- [ ] Cream of chicken
- [ ] Cream of mushroom
- [ ] Cream of onion
- [ ] Cream of potato
- [ ] Cream of shrimp
- [ ] Fiesta nacho cheese
- [ ] French onion soup
- [ ] Soups for when you need to "heat & eat"

- [ ] Tomato bisque
- [ ] Tomato soup
- [ ] _____
- [ ] _____
- [ ] _____

Canned Vegetables

- [ ] Artichoke hearts
- [ ] Asparagus (cut, spears)
- [ ] Bamboo shoots
- [ ] Beans
  - [ ] Black
  - [ ] Black-eyed peas
  - [ ] Cannellini
  - [ ] Garbanzo (chick-peas)
  - [ ] Great northern
  - [ ] Kidney
  - [ ] Lentils
  - [ ] Navy
  - [ ] Pinto
  - [ ] Split peas
- [ ] Beets
- [ ] Capers
- [ ] Carrots

- [ ] Chili beans
- [ ] Chop suey vegetables
- [ ] Corn
  - [ ] Cream-style
  - [ ] Mexicorn®
  - [ ] Shoe-peg
  - [ ] White
  - [ ] Yellow
- [ ] French-fried onions
- [ ] German potato salad
- [ ] Green beans (cut, French style)
- [ ] Green chilies
- [ ] Hearts of palm
- [ ] Italian green beans
- [ ] Jalapenos
- [ ] Lima beans
- [ ] Mixed vegetables
- [ ] Mushrooms
- [ ] Potatoes (sliced, whole)
- [ ] Pumpkin
- [ ] Roasted red peppers
- [ ] Sauerkraut
- [ ] Spanish rice
- [ ] Spinach

- [ ] Succotash
- [ ] Sweet peas
- [ ] Sweet potatoes (yams)
- [ ] Three bean salad
- [ ] Tomato sauce/puree/paste
- [ ] Tomatoes
  - [ ] diced
  - [ ] Mexican stewed
  - [ ] Italian stewed
  - [ ] stewed
  - [ ] sun-dried,
  - [ ] whole
- [ ] Tomatoes and green chilies
- [ ] Water chestnuts (sliced, whole)
- [ ] Wax beans
- [ ] Zucchini
- [ ] _____
- [ ] _____
- [ ] _____
- [ ] _____
- [ ] _____
- [ ] _____

Cereals

☐ Cream of wheat
☐ Dry cereal
☐ Grits
☐ Instant hot cereal packets
☐ Oatmeal
☐ _____
☐ _____
☐ _____

Chips & Snacks

☐ Candy
☐ Corn chips
☐ Dips & salsas
☐ Nuts/seeds
☐ Popcorn
☐ Potato chips
☐ Snack cakes
☐ Tortilla chips
☐ _____
☐ _____
☐ _____

☐ _____
☐ _____

Condiments & Spreads

☐ Honey
☐ Horseradish
☐ Hot red pepper sauce
☐ Jelly
☐ Jams & Preserves
☐ Ketchup
☐ Mayonnaise\
☐ Mustard (dijon-style, honey, yellow)
☐ Olives (green, black)
☐ Onions, pickled
☐ Peanut butter (creamy, crunchy)
☐ Pesto
☐ Pickles (dill, gherkins, bread & butter)
☐ Pickle relish
☐ Salad cream
☐ Salad dressings (Catalina, Caesar, French, honey-mustard, Italian, poppy seed, ranch, Russian)
☐ Salad dressing mixes

☐ Salsa
☐ Syrup (pure maple, flavored)
☐ Vinegar (cider, wine, white, balsamic, tarragon)
☐ _____
☐ _____
☐ _____
☐ _____
☐ _____

Cookies & Crackers

☐ Cookies
☐ Crackers (saltines, graham, specialty)
☐ _____
☐ _____

Instant Canned Meals

☐ Chili with beans
☐ Chili without beans
☐ Deviled beef, chicken, ham
☐ Hearty soups
☐ Pork and beans

☐ Sloppy Joe sauce
☐ _____
☐ _____
☐ _____

Sauces & Flavorings

☐ Alfredo sauce
☐ Barbecue sauce
☐ Bouillon – granules, cubes (chicken, beef, vegetable)
☐ Browning sauce
☐ Chili sauce
☐ Clam juice
☐ Cranberry sauce (jellied, whole berry)
☐ Fish sauce
☐ Gravy (jars, mixes)
☐ Hoisin sauce
☐ Hot red pepper sauce
☐ Ice cream toppings (butterscotch, caramel, fudge, fruit flavors)
☐ Liquid smoke
☐ Marinara sauce
☐ Oyster sauce

- [ ] Pizza sauce
- [ ] Sauce and seasoning mixes (chili, gravies, hollandaise, taco)
- [ ] Soy sauce
- [ ] Spaghetti sauce
- [ ] Steak sauce
- [ ] Stir-fry sauce
- [ ] Sweet-and-sour stir-fry sauce
- [ ] Teriyaki sauce
- [ ] Worcestershire sauce

- [ ] _____
- [ ] _____
- [ ] _____

Spices, Herbs & Extracts

- [ ] Allspice (ground, whole berries)
- [ ] Aniseed
- [ ] Basil
- [ ] Bay leaves
- [ ] Boils (shrimp, crab, fish)
- [ ] Caraway seeds
- [ ] Cardamom
- [ ] Celery seeds
- [ ] Chili powder
- [ ] Chives, dried
- [ ] Cinnamon (ground, sticks)
- [ ] Cloves (ground, whole)
- [ ] Coriander (ground, seeds)
- [ ] Creole seasoning
- [ ] Cumin (ground, seeds)
- [ ] Curry powder
- [ ] Dill weed
- [ ] Extracts (vanilla, almond, hazelnut, maple, peppermint, lemon, orange, other fruits)
- [ ] Fennel seeds
- [ ] Garlic powder
- [ ] Garlic salt
- [ ] Ginger (crystallized, ground)
- [ ] Italian seasoning
- [ ] Juniper berries
- [ ] Mace
- [ ] Marjoram
- [ ] Mint
- [ ] Mustard (ground, seeds)
- [ ] Nutmeg (ground, whole)
- [ ] Onion, dry flakes

☐ Oregano
☐ Paprika
☐ Parsley flakes
☐ Pepper and peppercorns (cayenne, dried red pepper flakes, white, black, green)
☐ Pickling spices
☐ Poppy seeds
☐ Pumpkin pie spice
☐ Rosemary
☐ Saffron threads
☐ Sage
☐ Salt (table. seasoned, coarse [kosher or sea salt])
☐ Savory
☐ Sesame seeds
☐ Tarragon
☐ Thyme
☐ Turmeric
☐ _____
☐ _____
☐ _____
☐ _____

Other

☐ Chow mein noodles
☐ Dried beans/lentils
☐ Gelatin (flavored, unflavored)
☐ Instant mashed potatoes
☐ Noodles
☐ Pasta, dried (angel hair, bow-tie [farfalle], elbow macaroni, fettuccine, lasagna, linguine, manicotti, penne, rigatoni, shell, spaghetti, wagon-wheel [rotini])
☐ Pudding mixes (cook & serve, instant)
☐ Ramen noodles
☐ Rice (arborio, basmati, brown, instant, white, wild)
☐ Rice mixes
☐ Soup mixes
☐ Stuffing mix
☐ Tortillas (corn, flour)
☐ _____
☐ _____
☐ _____
☐ _____

Produce

Buying Fresh Fruit and Vegetables

The prices are lowest at the peak of the harvest – and the produce is at its best quality! Plan your menus around what is available at its best price. Stock up if you can and freeze for later use.

Fresh Fruit

- [ ] Apples (cooking, eating)
- [ ] Apricots
- [ ] Bananas
- [ ] Blackberries (dewberries, boysenberries) Cherries
- [ ] Blood Orange
- [ ] Blueberries
- [ ] Cherries (sweet, black, tart)
- [ ] Citron
- [ ] Clementines
- [ ] Coconuts
- [ ] Cranberries
- [ ] Currants
- [ ] Dates
- [ ] Figs
- [ ] Grapefruit
- [ ] Grapes
- [ ] Guava
- [ ] Huckleberries
- [ ] Kiwifruit
- [ ] Kumquats
- [ ] Lemons
- [ ] Limes (Key, Persian)
- [ ] Lingonberries
- [ ] Loquats
- [ ] Mandarin oranges
- [ ] Mangoes
- [ ] Melons (cantaloupe, honeydew, muskmelon, Persian, watermelon))
- [ ] Oranges
- [ ] Papayas
- [ ] Passion fruit
- [ ] Peaches
- [ ] Pears

☐ Pineapple

☐ Plums

☐ Pomegranates

☐ Raspberries

☐ Strawberries

☐ Tangerines

☐ _____

☐ _____

☐ _____

☐ _____

☐ _____

Fresh Vegetables

☐ Artichokes

☐ Arugula

☐ Asparagus

☐ Avocados

☐ Bamboo shoots

☐ Bean sprouts

☐ Beans

☐ Beets

☐ Bell peppers (green, orange, red, yellow)

☐ Black-eyed pea

☐ Bok choy

☐ Broccoli

☐ Broccoli rabe

☐ Brussels sprouts

☐ Cabbage (green, red, napa/chinese)

☐ Carrots

☐ Cauliflower

☐ Celery

☐ Chickpeas

☐ Chili peppers

☐ Chives

☐ Cilantro

☐ Collard greens

☐ Corn on the cob

☐ Cucumbers

☐ Eggplant

☐ Endive

☐ Garlic

☐ Ginger

☐ Green beans

☐ Green onions

☐ Jerusalem artichoke

☐ Jicama

- [ ] Jerusalem artichoke
- [ ] Kohlrabi
- [ ] Leeks
- [ ] Lettuce (leaf varieties, head varieties)
- [ ] Mushrooms
- [ ] Mustard greens
- [ ] Okra
- [ ] Onions (red, sweet, white, yellow)
- [ ] Parsley
- [ ] Parsnips
- [ ] Peanuts
- [ ] Potatoes (baking, boiling)
- [ ] Prickly pear (nopales)
- [ ] Pumpkin
- [ ] Radicchio
- [ ] Radishes
- [ ] Rhubarb
- [ ] Rutabagas
- [ ] Scallions
- [ ] Shallots
- [ ] Spinach
- [ ] Squash (summer, winter)
- [ ] Sugar-snap peas

- [ ] Sweet peas
- [ ] Sweet potatoes
- [ ] Swiss chard
- [ ] Tomatillos
- [ ] Tomatoes (cherry, market, plum, romano)
- [ ] Turnip greens
- [ ] Turnips
- [ ] Vanilla beans
- [ ] Water chestnuts
- [ ] Watercress
- [ ] Yams
- [ ] Zucchini
- [ ] _____
- [ ] _____
- [ ] _____
- [ ] _____
- [ ] _____
- [ ] _____
- [ ] _____
- [ ] _____

Convenience Vegetables

Already chopped, shredded, peeled, and/or mixed make these great time savers, but they have a shorter shelf life than whole vegetables. Select only what you plan to use within their expiration date.

- [ ] Baby spinach
- [ ] Bell peppers (green, yellow, orange, red)
- [ ] Broccoli florets
- [ ] Carrots
- [ ] Onions
- [ ] Salad greens
- [ ] Slaws (cabbage, broccoli)
- [ ] _____
- [ ] _____
- [ ] _____
- [ ] _____

Dried Fruits & Other

- [ ] Apricots
- [ ] Apples
- [ ] Cranberries (Craisins®)
- [ ] Currants
- [ ] Mushrooms, dried – shiitake, porcini, morsels
- [ ] Nuts/Seeds
- [ ] Pears
- [ ] Prunes
- [ ] Raisins (dark, golden)
- [ ] _____
- [ ] _____
- [ ] _____
- [ ] _____

Bakery

- [ ] Bagels
- [ ] Bread (French, Italian, multi-grain, pumpernickel, raisin, rye, white, whole wheat)
- [ ] Breadcrumbs (seasoned, unseasoned)
- [ ] Cakes (angel food, pound)
- [ ] Cookies
- [ ] Croissants
- [ ] Croutons (flavored, unflavored)
- [ ] Doughnuts
- [ ] French Bread
- [ ] Hamburger buns
- [ ] Hot dog buns
- [ ] Muffins
- [ ] Pastries
- [ ] Pies
- [ ] Rolls
- [ ] _____
- [ ] _____

Deli

- [ ] Beef
- [ ] Cheese
- [ ] Chicken
- [ ] Dips
- [ ] Ham
- [ ] Main dishes
- [ ] Prepared salads
- [ ] Rotisserie chicken
- [ ] Salads
- [ ] Sandwich meats
- [ ] Side dishes
- [ ] Turkey
- [ ] _____
- [ ] _____
- [ ] _____

Dairy & Refrigerated Foods

- [ ] Biscuits
- [ ] Butter (salted, unsalted)
- [ ] Cheeses (shredded, sliced, whole, spreadable)
  - [ ] American
  - [ ] cheddar
  - [ ] colby
  - [ ] four-cheese blend
  - [ ] longhorn
  - [ ] Monterey Jack
  - [ ] mozzarella
  - [ ] parmesan
  - [ ] provolone
  - [ ] ricotta
  - [ ] romano
  - [ ] Swiss
  - [ ] Velveeta®)
- [ ] Cookies
- [ ] Cottage cheese (large curd, small curd)

- [ ] Cream cheese
- [ ] Creams (whipping cream, half-and-half, coffee creamers)
- [ ] Dips
- [ ] Eggs, large (baking recipes always use large eggs)
- [ ] Orange juice
- [ ] Margarine
- [ ] Milk (whole, skim, 2%)
- [ ] Pasta
- [ ] Piecrusts
- [ ] Pudding
- [ ] Sour cream
- [ ] Yogurt
- [ ] Pasta
- [ ] Rolls
- [ ] Spreadable butter/margarine
- [ ] Tofu
- [ ] Yogurt (flavored, plain)
- [ ] _____
- [ ] _____
- [ ] _____
- [ ] _____

Fresh Meats & Seafood

- [ ] Beef
  - [ ] Brisket
  - [ ] Ground
  - [ ] Roast
  - [ ] Steak
  - [ ] Tenderloin
- [ ] Chicken
  - [ ] Breasts (skinless boneless)
  - [ ] Drumsticks
  - [ ] Thighs
  - [ ] Whole
  - [ ] Wings
- [ ] Cornish hens
- [ ] Hot dogs
- [ ] Lamb (chops, leg, saddle)
- [ ] Pork
  - [ ] Bacon
  - [ ] Chops
  - [ ] Ground
  - [ ] Ham
  - [ ] Ribs
  - [ ] Roast
  - [ ] Sausage (bulk, link, smoked, Italian, other specialty sausages)
  - [ ] Tenderloin
- [ ] Sandwich meat
- [ ] Seafood
  - [ ] Clams
  - [ ] Crabs
  - [ ] Fish fillets or steaks
  - [ ] Lobsters
  - [ ] Oysters
  - [ ] Scallops
  - [ ] Shrimp
- [ ] Turkey
  - [ ] Breast
  - [ ] Ground
  - [ ] Tenderloin
  - [ ] Whole
- [ ] _____
- [ ] _____
- [ ] _____
- [ ] _____

Frozen Foods

Frozen Fruits

- [ ] Blackberries (sweetened, unsweetened)
- [ ] Blueberries (sweetened, unsweetened)
- [ ] Peaches (sweetened, unsweetened)
- [ ] Raspberries (sweetened, unsweetened)
- [ ] Strawberries (sweetened, unsweetened)
- [ ] _____
- [ ] _____
- [ ] _____
- [ ] _____

Frozen Desserts

- [ ] Cakes
- [ ] Ice Cream
- [ ] Pastries
- [ ] Pies
- [ ] Whipped topping

- [ ] Yogurt
- [ ] _____
- [ ] _____
- [ ] _____
- [ ] _____

Frozen Juices

- [ ] Grape
- [ ] Grapefruit
- [ ] Lemonade
- [ ] Limeade
- [ ] Orange
- [ ] Pineapple
- [ ] _____
- [ ] _____
- [ ] _____
- [ ] _____

Frozen Meals

- [ ] Breakfast
- [ ] Dinners/lunches
- [ ] Pizza

☐ Waffles

☐ _____

☐ _____

☐ _____

☐ _____

Frozen Vegetables

☐ Asian vegetable blends

☐ Asparagus

☐ Bell peppers and onions (seasoning blend)

☐ Black-eyed peas

☐ Broccoli (chopped, florets, spears)

☐ Brussels sprouts

☐ Carrots

☐ Cauliflower – florets

☐ Corn (cream-style, on the cob, white, yellow

☐ Green beans – whole, cut, French style

☐ Hash-brown potatoes

☐ Lima beans

☐ Mixed vegetables

☐ Potatoes

☐ Seasoning blend (bell peppers and onions)

☐ Spinach (cut leaf, whole leaf)

☐ Squash (summer, winter)

☐ Stir-fry vegetables

☐ Sugar snap peas

☐ Sweet peas

☐ White pearl onions

☐ Zucchini

☐ _____

☐ _____

☐ _____

☐ _____

Frozen Other

☐ Breads

☐ Ice

☐ Meats

☐ Piecrust

☐ Pizzas

☐ Seafood

☐ _____

☐ _____

Index

O

P

T

U

V

W

Z

Cookbooks Published by
Cookbook Resources, LLC
Bringing Family and Friends to the Table

Easy Diabetic Recipes	*Easy Potluck Recipes*
The Best of Cooking with 3 Ingredients	*Easy Casseroles*
The Ultimate Cooking with 4 Ingredients	*Easy Desserts*
Easy Cooking with 5 Ingredients	*Sunday Night Suppers*
Gourmet Cooking with 5 Ingredients	*Easy Church Suppers*
4-Ingredient Recipes for 30-Minute Meals	*365 Easy Meals*
Essential 3-4-5 Ingredient Recipes	*365 Easy Soups and Stews*
The Best 1001 Short, Easy Recipes	*365 Easy Vegetarian Recipes*
1001 Fast Easy Recipes	*365 Easy Chicken Recipes*
1001 Community Recipes	*365 Easy Soup Recipes*
Busy Woman's Quick & Easy Recipes	*365 Easy One-Dish Recipes*
Busy Woman's Slow Cooker Recipes	*365 Easy Pasta Recipes*
Easy Slow Cooker Cookbook	*365 Easy Slow Cooker Recipes*
Easy One-Dish Meals	*365 Easy Casserole Recipes*

Quick Fixes with Cake Mixes

Kitchen Keepsakes/More Kitchen Keepsakes

Gifts for the Cookie Jar

All New Gifts for the Cookie Jar

Muffins In A Jar

The Big Bake Sale Cookbook

Classic Tex-Mex and Texas Cooking

Classic Southwest Cooking

Miss Sadie's Southern Cooking

Texas Longhorn Cookbook

Cookbook 25 Years

A Little Taste of Texas

A Little Taste of Texas II

Trophy Hunters' Wild Game Cookbook

Recipe Keeper

*Leaving Home Cookbook
and Survival Guide*

Classic Pennsylvania Dutch Cooking

Healthy Cooking with 4 Ingredients

Simple Old-Fashioned Baking

**cookbook
resources**® LLC

www.cookbookresources.com

Your Ultimate Source for Easy Cookbooks

BUSY WOMAN'S
Quick & Easy Recipes
Make 'em Happy. Fix it Fast!

cookbook resources® LLC

www.cookbookresources.com